Advance Praise for
Realistically Ever After

"Reading Cristina is like having a personal conversation with a very wise friend—who's also very funny!"

  —Henry Winkler

"In this candid book, beloved television personality and former model Cristina Ferrare steps off the magazine covers to bravely reveal the truth behind the fairy-tale image of her life. In so doing, she shows us all that the quest for a life without warts and wrinkles—for the "happily ever after"—is futile. The truth is, there are no magic answers, but what life offers instead is ultimately much more satisfying."

  —Dr. Drew Pinsky, cohost of the nationally syndicated radio show *Loveline* and author of *Cracked: Putting Broken Lives Together Again*

"Any woman who is insecure about careers, sex, marriage, childbirth, raising children, or teenaged angst must read this book to know she's not alone. With candor and explicit detail, talented, beautiful, and successful Cristina lays bare her own insecurities and how to conquer them."

  —Nina Blanchard, modeling agent and founder of the Nina Blanchard Agency

"Woody Allen once said that he hates reality, but it's still the best place to get a good steak. What Cristina has shown us is that it is also the only place you can find lasting love, meaning, fulfillment, and the reality of God. She has done a great job of sharing the kinds of lessons we need in order to make marriage, kids, and real life a wonderful meal, even if it is not what we ordered."

  —Henry Cloud, Ph.D., author of *Boundaries* and *How People Grow*

REALISTICALLY
EVER AFTER

CRISTINA
FERRARE

REALISTICALLY EVER AFTER

Finding Happiness

When He's Not Prince Charming,

You're Not Snow White,

Life's Not a Fairy Tale

RODALE

Printed in the United States of America
Rodale Inc. makes every effort to use acid-free ∞, recycled paper ♻.

Photographs on pages xiv, 10, 22, 38, 50, 84, 102, 130, 148, 158 courtesy of Cristina Ferrare.

Photographs on pages 66 and 188 © Alex Berliner
Photograph on page 174 © Charles Bush

Book design by Judith Stagnitto Abbate/Abbate Design

Library of Congress Cataloging-in-Publication Data

Ferrare, Cristina.
    Realistically ever after : finding happiness when he's not Prince Charming, you're not Snow White, and life's not a fairy tale / Cristina Ferrare.
       p.   cm.
    ISBN 1–57954–947–0 hardcover
    1. Ferrare, Cristina. 2. Mothers—Biography. 3. Wives—Biography.
4. Models (Persons)—Biography. 5. Marriage. 6. Family. 7. Parenting.
I. Title.
HQ759.F43   2004
306.874'3'092—dc22   2003026819

Distributed to the book trade by St. Martin's Press

2 4 6 8 10 9 7 5 3 1 hardcover

RODALE
WE **INSPIRE** AND **ENABLE** PEOPLE TO IMPROVE
THEIR LIVES AND THE WORLD AROUND THEM

FOR MORE OF OUR PRODUCTS
WWW.RODALESTORE.COM
(800) 848-4735

To my mother Renata; my sister Diana; my daughters Kathryn,
Alexandra, and Arianna; my step-daughter Anne;
my nieces Danielle and Nickie; and my granddaughters
Claire and Acacia Rene.

Acknowledgments

First and foremost, I acknowledge that everything wonderful in my life comes from the grace of God. Everything that has been a challenge, difficult, and even tragic has been a blessing even when I didn't feel it to be so. It was during those trying times that He has been my biggest champion.

To my wonderful, patient, saint of a husband. No matter what harebrained idea I came up with, you always met it with the utmost support, respect, and encouragement. Never once did you discourage me. You always let me follow my dreams no matter how unlikely, impossible, or financially risky they were. There is a sign with a quote on a building looming high over Los Angeles next door to your beloved Greek Church, Saint Sophia's. It always reminds me of you. It is of two people embracing, holding each other up. The quote reads: "We are all angels with one wing. In order to fly, we must embrace each other." I can't wait to see where we're flying to next!

To Jan Miller, who is first and foremost my dearest friend. I met Jan eight years ago when I was searching for a literary agent. She agreed to take me on as a client when I had this idea that I could sit down and write a book. Not only did she take me on, her tireless effort and her encouragement helped me realize and nurture a passion

I had hidden deep down inside but was afraid to face: writing. It has opened up a whole new world! It changed my life.

Nothing has changed me more than having this incredible woman in my life. Jan, I have never known anyone quite like you. Through you, I have learned to breathe all over again taking in only good air. You are an important part of my life, one that I will cherish always. We are truly family, and to me that is everything! (I love your guts, girlfriend!)

I want to say thank you to my children, Zachary, Kathryn, Alexandra, and Arianna. You are my whole world and the reason I love life. Thank you for your support and encouragement as you watched your "crazy mother" go through so many different changes. The one thing that never changed was my deep love and commitment to you. I love being your mother! I'm also exhausted!

To my stepchildren, Annie, Denis, Mark, and son-in-law Patrice: I want you to know how much I love you and how important you are in my life. I wish I could take the credit for the way you turned out, but of course I can't. At least I can enjoy the results. I love you very much.

To my grandchildren, Claire, Kevin, and Acacia. I thought it was impossible to love anything as much as you love your own children until I had grandkids! I love them even more, and it is deliciously overwhelming!

I want to acknowledge the other extraordinary women in my life. It is from them and their strength of character, resolve, compassion, and loyalty that I can get through my day no matter what happens. I've taken examples from each and every one of them. Through them I've become a better wife, mother, daughter, sister, friend, and, most of all, a better person. I finally realize and can say with conviction, "I must be quite all right if these women can love me and be there for me unconditionally." What a gift, thank you for being there.

First and foremost, my mother, Renata, whose shining example has been a constant inspiration to me from the time I opened my eyes to see her smiling face.

My little sister Diana, who somehow has become the big sister. You always had wisdom beyond your years. You are a source of great comfort, and the amount of respect and love I have for you is endless!

My girlfriends, whom I cherish with all my heart, in order of appearance in my life: Susana Kobritz, Nina Blanchard, Eileen Burns, Anne Thomopoulos, Margaret Weitzman, Jimmie Ritchie, Genevieve Reitman, Maria Shriver, Nadine Schiff, Wanda McDaniel, Jan Miller, Heidi Krupp, Annie Gilbar, Evelyn Heyward, Linda Hogobian, Dru Hammer, Susan Cohn, Michele Girade, and Janet McGreal.

To Mark Seal, my friend, an extraordinary writer, and author who worked patiently with me to help me bring this manuscript up to speed. Your guidance was so appreciated. If you weren't such a hunky guy, you would make a great girlfriend!

I want to say a really big thank you to all of the wonderful people at Rodale for their support and for giving me a chance to keep reaching for my dreams, especially Tami Booth, Amy Rhodes, Cindy Ratzlaff, Cathy Gruhn, Lois Hazel, Trish Field, Judy Abbate, Joanna Williams, and Wendy Hess.

A special thanks to Amy Kovalski, my book editor, whose invaluable help shaped this book. Thank you so much, Amy, for helping me keep my voice while improving so much on the message that I'm trying to get across. It was a pleasure working with you.

Contents

One of the best memories of my dream home was the day
I brought baby Arianna home from the hospital.
Her sister, Alexandra, doesn't look so certain.

Introduction

I t was my dream home. But now, after eighteen years, which have been the happiest and most fulfilling years of my life, we are selling our house. And we must be out in thirty days!

This home, and the surrounding canyon, are the stuff that dreams are made of. The house sits deep in a canyon in one of the most beautiful spots in Los Angeles. It is a place full of a rich history of lush, flowering landscapes. About a mile down the hill is one of the world's most prestigious hotels, Hotel Bel Air. It's a tranquil sanctuary favored by royalty, heads of state, and movie stars, who revel in the hotel's luxurious surroundings, great service, and—most important—privacy.

Our house had come with a bit of Hollywood history. Built in 1932, it was once the home of legendary movie stars Betty Grable and her bandleader husband, Harry James. At least that is what the real estate agent told us. But I didn't believe it until I saw a photograph of them standing in front of the glass and brick greenhouse on the

1

back patio. It seemed so strange to see them surrounded by deep fuchsia-colored bougainvillea, flowering gardenias, and ripe fruit trees, actually standing in what were now "our" gardens.

The first time I drove through the large, wrought iron gates and up the well-traveled brick driveway, I was immediately struck by the grandeur of the huge old oaks with their gnarled branches reaching over the top of the ivy-covered brick Tudor. The ancient trees loom over the house as if they are protecting its occupants from intruders. They stand tall and sturdy, with a maturity about them that makes you feel safe. It looks like something out of a fairy tale.

The air is filled with the smell of orange blossoms and jasmine— the aroma so heady that it makes you stop, close your eyes, and inhale deeply. As you do, an overwhelming feeling of well-being rushes over you like a mini tranquilizer.

In this fairy-tale house, with my fairy-tale husband and our fairy-tale family, I planned to live out the rest of my life. I believed in fairy tales. They come true . . . *right?* I had evidence of it, right in my own backyard.

Yet as much as I truly loved our home, it had started to overwhelm me. I had been thinking, and mentioning, for some time that I wanted to change the way we'd been living. I just couldn't handle the upkeep any more. In my mind, everything in our home had to be picture perfect. When it wasn't, I'd become frustrated and disappointed. I felt that I wasn't able to maintain the kind of home I thought we should have—a home where the beds are always made, the dishes clean and stacked neatly in the cupboards, the bathrooms spotless, and the laundry clean and fresh-smelling. And that was only the inside of the house. On top of that, the gardens had to be constantly tended, weeded, reseeded, and planted.

Plus, there were the incessant demands of carpooling, grocery shopping, and cooking. And there were things that constantly went wrong with a house as old as ours. I wanted something smaller with less responsibility and lower maintenance. I wanted to make my life simpler.

My chance came on January 2, 2003. My daughters, Alexandra and Arianna, and I were heading home from the beach while my husband, Tony, ran some errands. We happened to drive by a newly built condominium complex. The building was so architecturally stunning that, on a whim, we decided to stop and take a look at some of the available units. We looked at several and thought they were nice, but nothing majestic, nothing magical. Sensing our lack of enthusiasm, the real estate agent suggested one more unit.

We rode the elevator up to the sky! When the doors opened and we stepped out, we were immediately struck by a panoramic view of the city I love. Up there, we could see Los Angeles, from the city to the mountains to the sea. My girls and I looked at each other.

"Wow, Mom, can we live here?" my younger daughter, Arianna, asked in awe.

"This is great!" added my older girl, Alex. "I feel like we're on top of the world! Come on, Mom, I know you've been thinking about making a change for a long time now. This is what you've been waiting for! Let's call Dad and see what he thinks!"

I was taken aback. It never occurred to me that the girls would consider moving out of the house they grew up in. Yet deep inside, I was secretly happy and relieved. I knew this was my chance to simplify my life, and I needed to take it.

But I had to be absolutely sure that my family would be all right with this big step. "Do you really want to do this?" I asked the girls sheepishly. "It would mean leaving the only home you have ever known. You need to think seriously about this."

I didn't want the moment to pass, so I added, "I don't know. What do you think? Should we call Dad to come up and see this?"

"Yes!" they both responded enthusiastically. "Let's call Dad!"

"He's going to love the doorman!" added Alexandra.

I called Tony.

"Meet us right away!" I said, giving him the address. "The girls and I have something very important we need to discuss with you."

Tony arrived twenty minutes later.

His first words were, "I love the doorman."

Then, rather suspiciously, he asked, "What are you girls scheming now?"

We all started to talk at once. Alex's voice rose above all of us as she simply stated in a tone that made Tony realize we were serious, "We want a change, Dad. We want to sell the house and move to this apartment in the sky!"

"It's time for a change!" added Arianna.

"You're serious, aren't you?" Tony asked. He looked out at the landscape sprawling in all directions below. "If this is what you guys really want, then I'm behind you 100 percent!"

He broke into a huge grin. "Let's do it!" he said.

Just like that, just that fast. Decision made, now we're moving. (Go figure.)

Our house sold the first week it was on the market (we were lucky), and the buyer wanted a thirty-day escrow. Moving eighteen years in thirty days? No problem. I can do it! *I'm Super Mom-Woman!*

For a month, I found myself stuck in a limbo of memories and moving vans. The dishes, furniture, and clothes were easy; pack 'em up and move 'em out. Every so often, though, amid the floor-to-ceiling moving boxes and utter chaos, with remnants of my life scattered about me with no semblance of anything that made sense, I'd stumble across family photographs. The pictures, which had been shoved into shoe boxes, shopping bags, and oversized plastic bags, seemed to have a life of their own, multiplying by the minute. Every time I'd empty out another closet or open another drawer, I'd find more. I found them just as I'd left them, along with all of my promises to buy leather-bound albums so I could have a chronological keepsake of our life together as a growing family.

We took a lot of family photos over the years. Whenever I would pick them up at the One Hour Photo, I would be excited and couldn't wait until we got home to look at them. I would find myself doing unsafe things like flipping through the pictures while driving or stealing a glance at a stop sign. When I got home, I would look at them once again to smile and reminisce. Then, inevitably, I would toss them on my desk. When the desk got too messy, I would transfer the photos to a drawer. Eventually, they would go into a box or plastic bag for safekeeping, along with my never-ending promises to someday put them into albums for the kids. But there was always so much to do. Slowing down long enough to lovingly place them in an album would never quite fit into my busy schedule.

So there I was, facing eighteen years of photos still waiting for their new home, with thirty days to move. I tried not to look through the photographs because I knew they would slow me down. But every time I'd come across a picture of the kids as babies, I'd pause and remember. I'd sit in awe and amazement at how little the girls were only yesterday. *What happened?*

One day, while I was sitting cross-legged on the floor, lost in another endless pile of photographs, Alex and Arianna came into the room. They began rummaging through the boxes and bags of photos, laughing and reminiscing about their life playing out before them.

Looking at a photo of herself at five with no teeth, Alex cringed. "Oh my gosh, look at how little I was!" she laughed. "I can't believe it. What a dork!"

Ari started to laugh as well, as she held up a picture of her much younger-looking father. "Think you look like a dork? Take a look at Dad in this picture!"

They both were laughing as they settled into rummaging through our life in a box.

"Gosh Mommy, look at how pretty you were," Alex said in wonderment, looking at a photo from my modeling days. *Ouch, that hurt.*

As we sifted through the photographs, I noticed something interesting. The pictures didn't tell the full story. The movers, I decided, would have to wait. I picked up the stacks of photographs and started telling my daughters my story—our stories—the fractured fairy tales that I had always painted with glitter, but that were, in reality, very different from what they seemed.

What I told my daughters that day became the basis for this book. I decided that as girls who would soon enough be young women, they needed to know that life is not always a fairy tale, the man you love may not always turn out to be Prince Charming, and being an adult can sometimes be downright disappointing or even scary. I knew that if only I had had a more realistic view of life as a young woman and mom, I might have saved myself a lot of heartache. Instead of expecting perfection (in myself and others), I could have reached for what is real and, ultimately, much more satisfying. And I knew that millions of other women needed to hear this message as well.

Still, let me make it clear that this book is not about the harsh realities in life. It's not about the threat of war, terrorism, racism, hunger, homelessness, gangs, rape, child abuse, sexual predators, illness, death, kidnappings, or school shootings. Trying to raise children safely in a global society faced with all this is real and frightening.

What we faced as a nation and a world after the events of September 11, 2001, forever changed the way we think and the way we now live our lives. We need to think twice about traveling (never mind how inconvenient it has become), and we are automatically suspicious of anyone who dresses or speaks differently than we do.

I don't forget for a second that life and the things that happen to us are real. After all, we are reminded of this by the news that plays in perpetuity. Headlines from all over the world are constantly bombarding us with images that have the power to be either disturbing or titillating.

I could go on and on about these harsh realities, but I won't. Instead, I would like to put them aside and present to you a simple and hopeful journey into what happens to you when you're out there simply living your life.

We all experience some pretty wonderful things. There are first kisses, proms, graduations, friends, engagements, weddings, anniversaries, babies, picnics, bike rides, art galleries, shopping, books, parties, museums, music, amusement parks, vacations, beaches, sports, movies, birthdays, family dinners, Thanksgiving, Christmas, television, presents, food, great restaurants, and infinite other wonderful things that make up one's journey through life. But despite all of these amazing things, life is far from a fairy tale.

From the moment that I could breathe, I believed in fairy tales. I wanted to live "happily ever after," and I sure went after it. From the career, to the man, to the house, to the kids—I was determined to have a storybook life. Yet, as you've already seen with my "dream house" that turned out not to be such a dream, I learned that life isn't always as it appears. Further, the events I depict are not exclusive to me. I'm sure you'll recognize yourself in a lot of the scenarios.

One of the dreams we all share is to marry Prince Charming, and to have our marriage last forever. Well, after three marriages, I can tell you what really happens after you repeat those immortal words, "For better or for worse." I experienced better, and it was nice. But the "worse" was really awful! When Prince Charming falls off his horse, it's not pretty. Imagine what it's like to have your husband arrested for allegedly selling coke (and I don't mean the soft drink). That's what happened while I was married to my second husband, John DeLorean. I'll tell you candidly what it's like to stand by your man. For now, let's just say that it wasn't as easy as I thought it would be.

I'll also give you an honest, behind-the-scenes look into having children. I'll discuss carrying them in your body for almost a year—and watching in amazement as you realize that your skin can actually stretch that much without tearing—giving birth to them, and then actually having to *raise* them.

Having kids might have been great if they didn't have to turn into *teenagers!* I thought having teenagers around the house would be a blast. The fact that I'm still alive after getting my first set of kids through their teens is a testament to the human survival instinct. And I still have two more to go! Who are these people, and why are they always so mad at you?

I'll also delve into the fine art of "blending families." Why does it look so simple on TV? Trying to be a stepparent and bring two families together as effortlessly as Carol Brady did on *The Brady Bunch* was something I thought I could pull off without a hitch, only to discover that I'm not that sweet, patient, or perky.

In fairy tales, there is nothing but sunshine and success. But in real life, there is a wicked witch called Failure.

I don't like to fail. It makes me feel awful, and then I eat a lot. Well, at least it did until I came to terms with it after a lot of soul-searching and one colossal disappointment. Does the search for Regis Philbin's new co-host ring a bell? I lost out on a job I had wanted with all my heart, and it took me a while to start moving again.

Yet that wasn't my first disappointment. Living in today's world meant I had to come to terms not with moving on, but with moving over. In the 1970s, I was considered a "supermodel." I was fortunate to be on the covers of all the major fashion magazines. But we all know that youth is what sells those magazines, and after a certain birthday, the calls don't come as frequently as they once did. In this book, I'll give you an insider's look into the so-called world of glamour and show you why I think it is a world built on potentially dangerous illusions.

It's my hope that these stories—which I refer to as fairy tales interrupted—will make you laugh and recall similar incidents in your own life. But most of all, I hope you will be able to put aside your own fairy-tale expectations and reach for something even better: your true self. You may not ride off into the sunset on a white horse, but you will discover how to live your life *realistically* ever after.

During the years I modeled, I thought I was living the
fantasy at home, too. Here I am in the apartment
John and I shared in New York.

CHAPTER 1

The Illusion of the Cover Photo

MY DAUGHTER ALEX interrupts my packing to tell me she has found a box with pictures from when I was modeling.

"Wow, Mommy, look how young you were," she says.

Now, *that* gets my attention. I take the photographs from her and there I am, forever young with flawless skin and sparkling blue eyes!

Seeing my picture in magazines was a thrill; being talked about in them was something else. It gave people carte blanche, or so they thought, to start talking to me when I least expected it.

I've gotten quite a bit of exposure over the years. I have appeared on the covers of *Harper's Bazaar, Cosmopolitan,* and numerous other fashion magazines. My television work co-hosting *AM Los Angeles,* substituting for Joan Lunden on *Good Morning America,* and co-hosting with Regis Philbin many times on *Live with Regis and Kathie Lee* made my face familiar to the public. Even today, people don't hesitate to approach me to talk. Wherever I go—the grocery store, airports, coffee houses, malls, you name it—people strike up conversations. They do so with such familiarity that it seems like we've been best friends since high school.

When you're on TV and magazine covers, people somehow feel that they know you. You share so many details of your personal life when you're on the air that when your audience meets you in person, they do the same!

I find it flattering that people talk to me about their careers, relationships, children, aging parents, and anything else that's on their minds. And believe me, people tell me *everything*, especially on the subject of sexual dysfunction. I wrote about the subject in my last book, *Okay, So I Don't Have a Headache*. It seemed to have touched a nerve across the country. All of a sudden, I became the poster child for Loss of Libido, even though I soon found it again.

It amazes me how much people are willing to share. Most of the conversations are rather graphic and deeply personal. It's actually pretty interesting stuff, but it's not fun when I'm trying to eat a meal.

A while back, I started noticing a common thread that ran through these chats. It became clear to me that most people were disappointed or confused that certain things in their lives—relationships, careers, even their families—hadn't turned out exactly as they thought they would. They had built up certain expectations, and they couldn't quite get over the fact that their lives had taken a different turn.

Women in airports who strike up conversations with me usually clutch their rolled-up women's magazines while confiding all kinds of disappointments and frustrations. I hear from heartbroken moms who are upset because their kids refuse to go to college. Some even break down and cry, like the woman who was at a loss as to why her precious baby girl who had made the honor roll was now in rehab. I also meet countless women who, after successful careers at huge companies with large paychecks and all the fringe benefits, are suddenly out of jobs. "And let's not forget how hard it was to get there in the first place," they'll say. Add to that the endless stories of sexual harassment, which is rampant, and tales of being passed over to make room for one of the "good ol' boys," which seems still to be the norm.

I just listen. That's all I need to do. After they unload what's on their minds, they go off to wait for their flights. I watch them sitting in the rows of airport chairs, passing the time by unrolling their women's magazines and flipping through the pages. They see glossy photo after glossy photo of women with flawless skin and size-two figures. They pore over the articles on how to have the perfect life, just like the flawlessly beautiful celebrity on the cover holding her two adorable, clean, well-dressed, well-behaved children. One child is always four, the other a newborn. The cover model sits there smiling with her immaculately manicured hands, beautifully styled hair, and a perfectly toned size two body that's already back to her pre-baby weight. The feature article is titled something like "How to Effortlessly Get Your Life (and Your Body!) Back After the Baby." *Yeah, right.*

We get sucked into that glossy magazine world from the get-go. We wonder how the featured celebrity so effortlessly segues from her nonstop TV career to being a hands-on mom and the perfect partner to her high-profile, high-paid, high-maintenance Power Husband. She also makes her own baby food (from scratch!) for her toddler and breastfeeds her infant between assignments. Then off she goes to "Mommy and Me" while making notes in the car for a book she is writing on how to raise well-adjusted kids. Wow! How does she do all of it and still look like *that?*

After reading articles like these, no wonder we feel like crap! Trying not to dwell on our inadequacies, we start to flip through the pages. Now we're bombarded with pictures of women—if you can call them that (most are just nineteen years old, and some are even younger)—in ads for everything from makeup to pantyhose, all looking incredible. The photos are so seductive we start to believe that we will be magically transformed into a gorgeous model if we buy what they're selling.

I once bought an outfit I saw in one of those fashion magazine ads. In my mind's eye, I actually thought the dress would fit me like it did the model. (My mind's eye needed glasses.) I thought that the dress was so beautiful that it would be just as stunning on me. *Oh my God! What was I thinking?!* Forget the fact that the dress the model had on was a size two. I ordered mine in a size ten, which should have been a twelve. It was slinky; she was slinky; I was not.

It was sad, actually. The dress style was really too young for me to begin with, but I totally bought into the whole image. *I wanted to be what I'd seen in the magazine.* I imagined I would look good in that dress. I reluctantly came to the conclusion and had to accept the fact that what we see on magazine covers and on their glossy pages is an illusion, a fairy tale.

Men buy into the fairy tale, too. I keep trying to explain to my husband, Tony, that after the Victoria's Secret models are finished shooting for the day, they're exhausted and just want to go home. They don't go flitting around their bedrooms in stilettos and a thong, ready to engage in full-throttle sex. All that most of them want to do is get a good night's sleep.

No one tells you what really goes on behind the façade of the advertising illusion, because the harsh reality would completely demolish the wonderful fairy tale. And, of course, it's the illusion that sells millions upon millions of dollars of clothing, cosmetics, and other merchandise each year. But it's also what sets up so many of us for disappointment.

I remember what it's like to be on the cover of one of those magazines, holding those perfectly adorable children. The cover photo was magical; I was beaming and my two children looked angelic. There was no hint of the chaos we all went through to get that one shot.

Here's the *real* story.

I get very little sleep the night before the cover shoot. The baby, Kathryn, wakes me up every two hours, but refuses to eat. When it's finally time to leave for the studio, she falls sound asleep. Of course, this makes us late for the photo shoot.

On top of that, I can't get my toddler out of bed because he wants to watch *Teenage Mutant Ninja Turtles* for the umpteenth time. I finally turn off the VCR and take him out of bed, kicking and screaming, and then try to get him dressed. He absolutely refuses. He hates the outfit, doesn't like the socks, and insists on wearing his dirty sneakers and the same underpants he wore yesterday because they have Ninjas on them. After bribing him with a trip to F.A.O. Schwartz for more Ninja turtles (I know, not good parenting, but I don't have time to worry about that right now), I take him to the kitchen to eat breakfast. He refuses to even touch his food.

I now have acid reflux because I'm so anxious about being late. The baby finally wakes up and won't do anything but scream until I feed her. After she's fed, I hand her to my mom to burp while I try to coordinate all of the gear I need to bring along to the photo shoot so the kids will have everything they need.

I look like hell. I have bags under my red, sleepless eyes.

Once we get to the taxi, Zach, the four-year-old, refuses to get into his car seat and settle down. What's worse, the baby squalls the whole way because *now* she has a giant, poopy diaper. The driver wants to kill me! To top it all off, it's morning rush hour traffic in Manhattan. Need I say more?

By the time I get to the studio, I want to kill myself. Now that we're nowhere near the breakfast table, my son is *starving* and wants to eat. When I go to have my makeup done, the photographer's assistants take him. I can hear his little voice screaming bloody murder. I see him trying the Ninja turtle moves on them to no avail. I try to pretend I don't hear my child's desperate cries.

As the makeup artist endlessly plucks and primps, my husband calls me at least nine times with his list of things I have to take care of before I get home. I'm trying to write everything down, but I have a difficult time hearing because the hairstylist is blowing my hair dry and managing to burn my scalp at the same time. I pull away from the heat, but the makeup artist gets all bent out of shape because my eyeliner is ruined from not sitting still. I now have liquid eyeliner stinging my eye, so my eyes begin to water, which makes my mascara run. I look like a raccoon that has been singed in a forest fire!

When I'm finally ready, I look at the time. It has taken ninety minutes to give me that natural, no-fuss, "cover girl" look! Of course I dare not laugh (who would want to by now, anyway?), eat, drink, or talk, because the ton of makeup that has been layered on my face to give me a porcelain peaches-and-cream complexion might crack, making me look like a map of the Sahara Desert.

Once we finally get into the photographer's studio and under the lights, it is nearly impossible to get the baby to simultaneously smile and keep her eyes open. She falls dead asleep in my arms, so I have no choice other than to put her down and let her nap. She does so, for two hours! Thank God I brought the Ninja Turtle tapes for Zach.

I change my blouse for the third time because heaven forbid there should be a wrinkle anywhere on the blouse. The stylists replace it with one that is crispy fresh. I wonder why they don't just retouch it like they do the wrinkles on my face. It makes me think that if they could, they would iron that, too.

Finally, everyone is awake, fed, and happy. Getting a picture with all of the elements in place is quite a challenge when there are kids involved. To have everyone smiling and looking in the same direction is a feat in itself. Every time I move the baby to hold her in a position where she doesn't look like a rolled-up wad of cotton, a team of hair-dressers, stylists, and makeup artists swoop in to do their thing be-cause, God forbid, a hair might be out of place.

By the time we finish, we have a beautiful photo for the cover, but only one. One single perfect photo out of six rolls of film and seven hours of hard work!

Three months later, the cover finally hits the newsstands. There I am, looking rested and beaming. My hair has that soft, flowing, ca-sual-but-stylish look that seems effortless and manageable. My eyes are bright and a perfect shade of sparkling blue that I don't recognize, because it's not mine but the photo retouching lab's addition of ac-cessory color. My face shows no signs of puffiness, also thanks to the lab. My blouse is wrinkle-free, and my two angelic children are sit-ting on my lap, smiling and looking adorable. There is absolutely no hint of the harsh reality of that long and tiresome photo shoot.

Only a few months later, our family will be embroiled in an in-ternational scandal (which I'll get into later). So much for perfection! At least we got the cover photo.

It may seem strange, but I still buy the women's magazines, de-spite the fact that I have spent years of my life on the "other side" and have seen firsthand what it takes to create the image of a magazine-perfect world. Though I know it takes special lighting, experienced makeup artists, and photo retouching to create such a world, I still find myself buying into the hype of those fairy-tale photos. We live in a time of nonstop bombardment from all sorts of media—magazines, television, radio, movies, books, and billboards—and it's very hard not to be seduced by what they're selling.

Madison Avenue would have you believe that if you wear certain clothes, purchase this toothpaste, drink that brand of liquor, or use these cosmetics, your life will be better. I was in those photo ads, and even *I* never looked that good—it's called retouching! My real life was nothing like the ads that I posed for.

Don't think that I don't want to be in that Ralph Lauren world; it would be a dream-come-true. I would love to be able to layer those fabulous clothes, or to wrap a sweater around my shoulders casually without looking like an Eskimo! Sitting next to a gorgeous, preppy guy in a speedboat, skimming along the water in Easthampton, would be just fine with me! His sun-streaked straight hair getting tossed by the wind and open shirt exposing his washboard stomach would float my boat any day! *(Where does Ralph Lauren get these people?)*

I would even settle for staring at Ralph Lauren in person. It would make my day just to gaze at him in his Stetson as he leans on his worn leather saddle by the barn, observing the polo matches. Just from looking at the photos, I can tell that he also smells divine!

In media land, everything is seductive. Magazines and TV commercials may be the media we see the most, but soap operas and movies play the same tricks on us. The lighting is always perfect, the settings are just right, and the people are gorgeous without a hair out of place.

When we watch the soaps, we forget about reality, even the reality of tiny details. I especially love those satin nightgowns the women wear in the love scenes. They slide off effortlessly, exposing smooth, freckle-free skin. Mine doesn't do that—it gets stuck along the way. I'd have to spray "Pam" all over my body to assure a smooth slide!

When TV characters writhe around in bed while making love, there's always music in the background. The music is intoxicating and sets the mood, a seductive melody that keeps pace with the couple's movements. Of course, the TV actors have a choreographer, professional sound engineer, and an editor to ensure that the music is perfectly in sync with their foreplay.

In real life, the song is only three and a half minutes. It ends long before anything has had time to develop. You either have to get up and start the song over again or be prepared to climax as soon as you hit the sheets.

And speaking of sheets, I'm always amazed at how those satin sheets on television remain so clean and strategically placed around special parts of the body. I don't know about you, but I need a giant down comforter to hide my body parts!

The actors on screen are able to get through a whole night's sleep wrapped in each other's arms without getting a stiff neck, and never stirring until morning. When they awaken, they can have a conversation with their faces a mere two inches apart, never once worrying about morning breath. His hands caress her stomach and she doesn't once complain about having to pee! Everyone is so buffed and shiny!

The weight-loss industry will have you believe that if you just lose a few pounds, Brad Pitt will leave Jennifer Aniston for you. You start believing that if you buy the right products, fix your hair the right way, and wear the right clothes, the new and improved you can actually change George Clooney's mind about remaining a bachelor forever!

Ah yes, if only I could lose the weight, if only my teeth were whiter, if only I drove that brand of car, if only I hung out with those people . . . if only, if only, if only!

Then I would be happy.

So here we are, as a society, trying to figure out how to fill this hole in our souls so we can feel better about ourselves. We're constantly made to feel we are missing something, and we grasp at anything that offers hope of making us feel complete. We are sure the solution that will bring us happiness is out there waiting for us, if only we search hard enough for it.

I got so desperately tired of trying to find out what it was I was missing! I read every self-help book on the market on how to improve my attitude, my relationships, my weight, my marriage, and my myriad careers. I have been searching in books for the meaning of life and for inner peace.

It seems like everyone is writing an advice book on how to cope with life. Just walk down the aisle of any bookstore, and you'll be bombarded with titles like these:

How to Love Yourself
I'm Okay, You're Not!
I'm My Mother!
Hug Me: I Have No Life
Find Inner Peace in Just Three Short Weeks
Find Yourself and Never Get Lost Again
Listening to Your Inner Child
How to Tell Your Inner Child to Leave You Alone!
Why Are You Fat?
It's Okay to Be Mad!
Why Are You Mad?
Who Are You Mad At Anyway?

Everyone has a point of view, so they write about it, go on tours to promote it, sell it, and give you solutions to your burning questions, chief of which is: *How can I have it all?*

If the topic strikes a chord, we purchase the book with the hope of finding answers. The problem is that you start out with the best of intentions and actually follow the advice for a few short days, or maybe even weeks. But then you slip back into your old ways, and you're back to feeling bad again and facing the same problems.

What if there are no solutions? What if we agree that there is only reality, and the reality is that we all share the same dreams, fears, and hopes in life? What if the reality is that we all have different paths with different stops along the way, but the road is the same? Some of us are dealt a heavier hand, and those people must recognize their need for help from friends, family, or professionals—and have the courage to get it. But in the end, there is no fairy tale for any of us, no matter what our tax bracket, job title, or address. And the truth is that real life is ultimately much more satisfying than the fairy tale anyway.

I believe we'd all be happier if we accepted that there are always going to be problems in life. Everyone has problems. You know what? *Your problems are not the problem.* The problem is all in how you *handle* what life throws at you.

After all, life is messy. It's full of difficulties: some minor, some scary. But dealing with them, and coming out the other side better for the experience, is all part of the wonderful process of reality.

As I gently place the photographs from my modeling days back in their box, I think of how my life has changed since then. There have been amazing moments of joy—marriages, babies, career successes—and incredible moments of heartache. But in the end, I wouldn't trade any of it—not even for Madison Avenue's idea of perfection.

My first job as a talk show host was with Steve Edwards on A.M. Los Angeles. I did the show for five years. Steve was the best teacher I ever had!

The Fear of Failure

LOOK, MOMMY, it's a picture from when you were on TV," says Arianna, fishing out another remnant of my life from the box of photographs.

She sifts through photos of me on various talk shows and then finds one of Regis Philbin and me marching in the St. Patrick's Day parade in New York City. He's wearing a kilt and I'm wearing a ridiculous-looking hat. We are walking arm-in-arm. We're smiling. We're obviously in cadence with the bagpipers marching behind us.

It all suddenly comes back in vivid color: The photo was taken during the time I was co-host for the week on the popular daytime TV show *Live with Regis and Kathie Lee*.

I was beaming!

Because this was my dream-come-true—except it didn't.

Looking at the picture makes me sad. It reminds me of my problem with fear of rejection and failure. This was, and remains, the biggest problem in my life.

Of course no one likes to fail. And failure is especially difficult to accept if the thing you fail at is something you've put a lot of time and effort into, or if it's something you really believe in. It can be devastating when your dream fails to turn out the way you had imagined.

However, after experiencing "failure" as often as I have, I realize that (although it sounds like a cliché) failure can actually be a good thing. If you rise above it and don't give up, failure always turns into something better.

But it sure feels awful while you're going through it.

When I was growing up, it never occurred to me that I wouldn't be able to attain all of my heart's desires. After all, didn't my parents tell me I could accomplish anything, if only I put my mind to it?

I certainly put my mind to a lot of things, but a lot of them just didn't turn out the way I wanted. So every time something didn't come out perfectly, I felt like a big fat failure. Why did it feel so bad to fail?

It took me many years to realize that I had a hard time accepting failure because I was never taught to fail. I was taught only how to win and succeed. Failure wasn't an acceptable option: It was to be avoided at all costs. Our culture cares only about winners and shuns failures. Winning is everything. People love winners! Everyone wants to be around winners!

Then you fail.

How can you feel anything *but* miserable? I don't know about you, but most of the people I know have never been taught how to deal positively with failure. As a result, we end up being fearful of doing anything that might get us branded a failure. But in our quest to become what society deems admirable, we start to lose bits and pieces of ourselves along the way. Our fear of being labeled a failure chips away at our self-esteem and self-worth. And then, when we do fail (as happens to everyone at some time), we lack the skills to deal with the failure in a way that helps us grow. Instead, we just feel awful.

It took me a long time to understand that when I failed at something or experienced a setback, things would eventually turn out okay. In fact, these "failures" would often turn out to be "good things"— building blocks for the soul, if you will.

One of these building blocks for my soul was when I failed to become the successor to Kathie Lee Gifford on *Live with Regis and Kathie Lee.* Of course, I didn't see it as a building block when it happened. It was more like a big brick that fell on my head.

When Kathie Lee announced her retirement, and it became well known that Regis was looking for a new co-host for the show, I naturally assumed (*never* assume anything) that I would be his obvious choice. After all, I had been a TV co-host for seven years, on and off, long before anyone was hosting morning television shows. I began co-hosting in the Stone Age, when it wasn't considered the hot thing to do. I assumed I would be the natural choice before anybody.

This was my dream job. Getting it represented reaching the pinnacle—working with Regis. I adored working with him, and it meant everything to me. I considered it to be my pot of gold at the end of the rainbow.

But then it didn't happen.

I'll get to why it didn't happen in a moment. But first I have to admit that I should have been prepared for it. Looking back now, I realize that it was only one of a string of seemingly bitter failures which, along with some measure of success, have comprised my life so far.

———— ✳ ————

As a girl, I had to study like crazy in order to get my hard-earned "C." Back when I started school, the concept of "learning challenged" was nonexistent. I had a very tough time memorizing information, which made school difficult for me. I thought I was dumb, and so did my teachers and classmates.

The situation did nothing to bolster my already fragile self-esteem, which led me to develop my lifelong battle with food. What eventually saved me was my hidden creative side, which was slowly emerging.

One afternoon I came home from school, frustrated and angry because my home economics teacher failed me in cooking class. Failed *me!* Me, the woman who would grow up to write a best-selling cookbook! How could she fail *me?* "Probably because you always interrupt her with suggestions on how to cook," my mother gently suggested.

I grew up in an Italian household. Our middle name was "Food." It was the one thing I was completely sure about. Food was the absolute in my life—the rock I lived on, surrounded by endless uncertainties. Cooking was something I knew with certainty. On the other hand, my teacher only seemed to know how to cook boring, stereotypical dinners: pot roast, mashed potatoes, and over-cooked green beans. Her dinner salad consisted of iceberg lettuce with Thousand Island dressing and a cherry tomato on top! Nothing wrong with that, but I had loftier ideas.

I suggested to her that we start our model dinner with angel hair pasta with fresh tomato sauce and fresh basil. It should be followed by chicken piccata in a lemon caper wine sauce, accompanied by sautéed spinach in olive oil and garlic with a squeeze of fresh lemon juice. To complete the dinner, we'd segue into a fresh garden salad with shaved Parmesan curls, dressed with olive oil and lemon juice.

This was the early sixties, when sauce came from a can and not from garden-fresh tomatoes. Chef Boyardee was king. Mediterranean and California cuisines hadn't been introduced yet, and Wolfgang Puck was a teenager living in Austria, which we couldn't even find on a map.

My teacher looked at me like I was from another planet! She would have none of my suggestions on cooking. But I refused to cook and eat her pot roast, potatoes, or iceberg lettuce salad.

So she failed me.

And my litany of failing began.

I didn't get credit for the home economics course, which meant that I had to go to summer school in order to graduate. If I couldn't graduate, I couldn't go to college to study to become a dietitian. That is what I wanted to become. I wanted to be an expert on food.

My dream was to open my own little shop where I could serve espresso coffee, homemade soups, fresh garden salads, and sandwiches on freshly baked French and Italian breads. I would also have the best homemade desserts in the world. As it turned out, I got sidetracked.

One afternoon, my mother was talking to a friend she had just met. After my mother introduced us, her friend said, "Cristina, you're a very pretty girl. Have you given any thought to a modeling career?"

"Not really," I shot back, "I'm still trying to figure out how to pass pot roast!"

"Excuse me?" she asked.

"Never mind," I sighed, still agitated at my home economics teacher.

After my snack of homegrown tomatoes with mozzarella and basil on toasted French bread drizzled with olive oil (Martha Stewart was still in college, but I was already obsessed), the woman and I started chatting about modeling.

"I could get you in to see Nina Blanchard," she said.

"Who?" I asked.

"Nina Blanchard," she said. "She's the leading modeling agent here in Los Angeles. Would you like to meet her?"

"Sure, why not," I said, figuring the extra money could help me with my college tuition.

I went to meet Nina Blanchard. Because I knew nothing, I expected nothing.

"Can you lose ten pounds?" she asked me.

"Piece of cake," I said.

"Well you won't be having that anymore," she shot back with a grin. She handed me a contract and signed me on the spot. The best thing to come out of our meeting was a lifelong friendship with this extraordinary woman.

Suddenly, I had been launched on a career path that I had neither considered nor even known about. An opportunity presented itself, and I went along for the ride. Meeting the woman who introduced me to Nina Blanchard changed the course of my life.

—— ✻ ——

I became a successful model rather quickly, so I thought everything in my life would be a slam-dunk. I was on the covers of all the leading fashion magazines, had a contract with cosmetics giant Max Factor, traveled the world, and made more money than I ever could have imagined. The idea of owning my own food shop was becoming a distant memory. I was being swept away into a new and exciting world! Modeling opened many doors for me.

One opportunity was a seven-year deal with movie studio 20th Century Fox. Fox was launching a talent department. I met with the studio heads, and, as Nina had done, they signed me on the spot. *Another slam-dunk!* All I had to do was show up Monday through Friday and take lessons in acting, singing, dance, mime, and elocution. For that, they would pay me a salary.

Four months into the program, I was sent on an audition at the rival MGM studio for a lead in a movie called *The Impossible Years*. The role was that of a seventeen-year-old high school girl who gives her parents nothing but trouble. *Perfect.*

I went along with the understanding that if I got the part, Fox would loan out my services to MGM, and I would continue to get my compensation from Fox. Sometimes ignorance is bliss. I had never auditioned for anything, nor had I acted in anything other than some scenes at Fox's studio.

I walked into the director's office. He didn't bother to say hello.

He took one look at me and boomed, just like they do in the movies, "This is it! This is the girl!"

Just like a fairy tale.

It was effortless.

———— ⚜ ————

You're probably wondering what all these easy successes have to do with failing. Wait.

Looking back, I now realize that having success handed to me so fast and so easily left me totally unprepared for the inevitable failure. I had been on such a smooth road that I never thought to brace myself for the bumps. All of us, at one point or another, will come to a bump in the road. Sometimes it's a big one. You might even encounter a hole so big you wonder how in the world you will ever crawl out of it.

I thought acting was the thing for me. I was absolutely sure that the entertainment business was something I wanted to be a part of. *The Impossible Years,* my first film, was a huge success. It opened at Radio City Music Hall in New York City at Christmastime, with the high-stepping Rockettes as part of the day or evening's entertainment packages. I thought I was on my way.

After that, I did two more movies and some television. I read for many things and thought that someone would feature me in another big movie. It never happened. To make a very long and painful story short, movie stardom was not my destiny. To be completely honest, while I did okay with my acting debut, I simply did not have the chops to be a good actor. I got thrown into a very big, very grown-up world with one of the largest studios behind me, and it was all so intoxicating that I wanted more. It was hard to let go.

Knowing when it was time to move on was a big step for me. It was hard to accept that I had come to the end of my movie career. Also, I was nervous because I wasn't prepared to do anything else besides modeling and acting. I wanted to keep working, but I was becoming "not bankable." After all, I was almost twenty-five! I was no longer considered a babe! *Ouch!*

I tried to find something to occupy my time while I looked for my next job, so I started painting. This was a talent I didn't know I had, and it brought me comfort and pleasure. I quickly became addicted to my painting, to the point of obsession. When I opened my eyes in the morning, I would make a beeline to my makeshift art studio—my kitchen table—and literally paint all day long. I wouldn't take phone calls because they would take me out of "my world." I felt safe there; no one could reject me or make me feel bad. I was happy, and the peace it afforded me was worth everything.

Yet when Hollywood finally knocked on my door again, I put my painting on hold. I just couldn't resist the allure, so I went back for more. This time, it was for talk shows.

I went through a succession of talk show gigs, including *A.M. Los Angeles, Home Show, Cristina & Friends, Home & Family,* and *Men Are from Mars, Women Are from Venus.* None of them ever made it to the big time, which is why you probably don't recognize any of the names. Each time I hoped for my turn to be a major player, and each time it didn't happen.

I also filled in as the guest co-host for many shows, including *Good Morning America, Live with Regis and Kathie Lee, The Vickie Lawrence Show,* and *Good Day Live.* I hung in there because I truly loved the work. I felt comfortable and at ease. I enjoyed meeting new people and interviewing them.

I had the opportunity to meet practically every major celebrity as they came on the shows to promote their latest project. I met stars in every field: medical experts, political leaders, heroic lifesavers, and more.

I particularly enjoyed working in front of a live audience. It was a thrill to walk out and have people respond with so much positive energy. Even if I was cranky or moody when I headed for work in the morning, by the time I finished doing the show, I felt great for the rest of the day, thanks to all the positive feedback from the audience.

I desperately wanted the talk show world to scoop me up and embrace me along with Phil Donahue and a then up-and-comer out of Chicago named Oprah Winfrey. Boy, was I in for a long haul.

I was also ultimately in for the biggest disappointment of my life.

———— ⁊ᛉ ————

The job that I loved more than anything else was co-hosting with Regis Philbin on *Live with Regis and Kathie Lee.* I filled in for Kathie Lee on a regular basis over the course of four years. That was the highlight of my film and television career. Even before I began guest co-hosting, I had been an enormous fan of the show and watched it religiously. I would dream of what it would be like to sit in Kathie Lee's chair and banter back and forth with that adorable Reege. Sometimes dreams do come true.

When Kathie Lee was expecting her first child, she planned to take a six-week maternity leave. I received "the call" from the show's producers: Would I be interested in filling in for Kathie Lee while she was away? *Are you kidding?* Of course! What a rush! I absolutely loved being back in New York and working with Regis. He was fun, open, generous, and the best person to bounce things off of! I felt completely at home and in my element with him on that show.

When Regis walked onstage, the audience would go nuts and the energy level was so high that you could ride the crest of excitement! It would carry you through the whole show and all the way through the rest of the day. I felt so alive and thrilled beyond words to have this incredible opportunity and to be working with Regis. The exhilaration of working with the live New York audience was like no other.

Tony and the kids came to New York to stay with me, and I was so happy. I was happy to be living in New York again, happy to have my family with me, happy to go to work every morning.

Over the next three years, I was asked to fill in for Kathie Lee on a regular basis, and I always jumped at the opportunity. When Kathie Lee announced to the world that she would be doing the unthinkable—*leaving* the show—I was eating my breakfast.

I nearly choked on my bran flakes.

I gasped along with the audience.

Then I panicked.

Oh my gosh, I thought, *this is it! I'm moving to New York!*

I was so darn sure that if Joy—Regis's lovely and talented wife—wasn't going to be his partner, I would be the next choice. After all, Regis and I had already established a rapport and were comfortable with one another. We knew each other's timing and shared a wealth of life experiences. It seemed—to me at least—a natural fit.

Sure enough, I received a call to come to New York and co-host the show for a day. I was thrilled and, for the first time, a little nervous. They were also having every person who had ever lived audition for the gig. It didn't make me nervous; I was a talk show host, I had years of experience doing live shows, Regis and I liked one another, and I naïvely thought there was no serious competition.

After the show was over, I felt exhilarated as always. I was excited about the possibility that this was going to be my new home. Finally, after all these years of short-term jobs, I felt that I was just steps away from realizing my dream. I looked around the set before I left and imagined myself in my new home.

My daydream didn't last long.

After the show, Michael Gelman, the producer of *Live,* walked into the dressing room as he always did. In the past, he had always been warm, sweet, talkative, and wonderful. This time, he was different. He barely looked me in the eyes. His normal friendly banter turned into a very businesslike, "Thank you, Cristina," as he pecked me on the cheek and disappeared down the short hall. I shut the door to Kathie Lee's dressing room, which I used while I was there. He didn't have to say anything more. I knew that my moment had passed, that in some way I had failed, that I wasn't getting the co-hosting job.

For a moment, I stood there staring at Kathie Lee's shoes still hanging on the back of the door. I took a deep breath and started counting the shoes, over and over. I don't know why. I just knew if I exhaled, I would cry.

As I gathered my things and looked around, I knew this would be my last time in that dressing room, my last time on that show. I headed out the door. There was no one out in the hall, so I left.

It was then that I realized that if I couldn't partner with Regis, there was no point in continuing down this road. It wasn't going to get any better than that.

I don't ever remember feeling so bad. The awareness that the talk show thing wasn't going to happen paralyzed me. It was another rejection, another disappointment, another failure. This one was too big for me to handle with grace and dignity.

How did I handle it? Not well, I must admit. First, I cried. In fact, I cried a lot. Next, I got angry. Then, I gained twelve pounds. I didn't return phone calls; I didn't want to see my friends because I thought they were all talking about me and my failure. I felt humiliated.

Then, in the midst of my biggest failure, I learned the secret of success.

─── ⚹ ───

Shortly after the Regis Rejection, which I concluded was the biggest failure of my life, I overheard a dinner conversation that changed my whole attitude about failure and fear of failure. Some guests were talking about different jobs they'd had. They talked about how they were fired from jobs they had thought they'd love and didn't get ones they coveted. All of them acknowledged how devastated they were to have "failed." But as they continued the conversation, they reached a surprising consensus: They all felt that in hindsight, whatever had happened was the best thing that could have happened. It forced them to move forward, take stock of themselves, and try new things. They ended up in jobs they loved, and they were now completely thrilled at the new and exciting directions in which their lives were heading.

Everyone seemed so genuine. Everyone had interesting tales to tell. Everyone had benefited from failure. That dinner conversation stuck in my head. I was curious to find out what people perceived as failure. I decided to talk to as many people as I could in order to learn their thoughts and get their insights on failure. I wanted to know how they dealt with failure in their lives, and how they managed to move forward. What I learned was interesting, thought provoking, and insightful.

I was so excited about my findings that I put it all together in an outline for a book. I wanted to call it *Failure: It's a Good Thing!* and I wanted it to present all the wonderful, perceptive, and encouraging stories I heard.

When I took my idea to my publisher, I was met by a barrage of "No's." I was told that no one wanted to read a book about failure. They reminded me that it has a negative connotation, and they said that anything with the word "failure" on the cover was a definite turn-off and would never become a bestseller. I was told people only wanted to read about positive things with happy endings. One member of the publishing house quoted something he'd read in the foreword of a book about success. "Do you know why there are no books about how to fail?" the foreword read. "Because everybody knows how to do it." They rejected the idea. I did not.

I continued to gather more information, and I came back with a different point of view. This time it was hopeful, focusing on the positive. Everyone I interviewed had interesting stories of failure and how it helped shape their outlook, personality, and—ultimately—the outcome of their lives.

Whenever I posed the question, "Have you ever failed at anything?" I got a resounding "Yes!" Everyone I interviewed had failed at something. Most of them had failed at many things. Everyone experienced frustration, anger, self-doubt, and low self-esteem. *What a relief! I wasn't alone in my feelings!*

More important than these feelings, though, is something nearly everyone confided to me. The common thread uniting these stories is that each person realized that once they accepted their failure, it turned out to be the best thing that could have happened to them.

If only I could have recognized sooner that my own setbacks were temporary. If only I could have kept the disappointments from overwhelming me. I could have saved *a lot* of calories and probably could have avoided the necessity of having one side of my closet reserved for fat clothes! You know what I mean—the side where all of the pants have elastic waistbands and the shirts and sweaters are all oversized?

Some people find their means to cope in booze or drugs. I find mine in food. I still struggle with this issue. Whenever I'm anxious, nervous, sad, or disappointed, my drug of choice is food. Not healthy food, of course, but bad food: anything greasy, crunchy, salty, or chocolaty. I don't understand to this day why I do it. I really try to control it, but it's bigger than me. I'm not going to pretend that this condition doesn't exist, it does. I have to deal with it on an almost daily basis.

I've failed at diets, I've been passed over for jobs I really wanted, and I've been hurt by people I love. So, yes, I have had my share of failures. I've experienced the lessons we're told we need in order to be a good sport, and all that other junk we're taught so we can pretend to be gracious when we lose. Guess what? I'm still having plenty of failures! Dealing with failure was hard in the past, and it's still hard. No matter what I read about self-esteem and how to cope, the bottom line is that we're human. We can work on the behavior, but we're still going to feel bad.

So even though failure still happens to me, now I have a better and healthier attitude about it. Of course, that's after I have a good cry, or a tantrum, after I get over thinking that I'm life's biggest loser, or after I go to the refrigerator and don't leave until it's empty of everything that's not fat- or sugar-free.

—— 🐎 ——

While I was watching the dial on the scale inch up following my Regis Rejection, I realized that I needed to get a grip on myself. I needed to set an example for my children and show them that you have to be tough, you have to move forward. I'd had my grieving time, and now it was time to start the healing.

I had to prove to them and to myself that you can't let setbacks and disappointments in life overtake your personality or chip away at the very core of your being. I had to show them that letting failure paralyze you, punish you, or pummel you with the refrigerator door is dangerous. The danger is getting comfortable with the feeling of feeling bad. Then you start to give yourself permission to act badly. I was acting badly.

Finally I learned that something good could come out of something bad. I realized that the first step is to accept that it's okay to feel bad and acknowledge that it hurts. After that acknowledgment, you have to get on with your life and not let the last failure—or the next one—bring you down. It's true that failures represent opportunities, and they have as much value as successes in terms of character development and experience building.

I still find it difficult to watch *Live*. It's not because I'm still angry or because I don't like Kelly Ripa, the person chosen to replace Kathie Lee. She's pretty, entertaining, and funny as hell. She is also young and perky, and people love her.

But watching the show reminds me that I've been replaced. It was really hard to get used to the idea that I had to move on or step aside. The question for me was how to go forward with my life in spite of the loss.

I instinctively knew I needed to tap into my creative talents. I remembered the joy and passion I had felt years earlier when I was painting. That was it: I needed to go inside, instead of outside myself to tap into something deep in my soul.

That realization was the beginning of greater things yet to come.

John DeLorean and I, living in our fake world. Why am I not smiling?

CHAPTER 3

When Prince Charming Falls Off His Horse

G EE, HOW OLD WERE YOU when you first got married, anyway?" Alex and Arianna ask in unison as they rummage through another box of photographs. They'd hit the mother lode of memories: my wedding albums—three of them to be exact.

"Well, as you know, girls, I've been married three times," I say. "Each time I took those vows, I meant every single word. I promised to honor and cherish, just as it's written. I was a young nineteen the first time I married. I didn't understand that the bonds of matrimony are held together by a spiritual commitment between two whole people coming into a union of mutual love, respect, and loyalty. All of this takes work and understanding because all of these virtues will be tested as time goes on, sometimes to the limit.

"On your wedding day, you repeat the words 'for better or for worse,' never anticipating how 'worse' worse can get. As you say those vows, you figure that whatever 'worse' is, you'll be able to deal with it because your love for each other is so deliriously heady and strong.

"You mutter—and I mean *mutter*—the words 'for poorer.' No one wants 'for poorer.' You gloss over it because it doesn't fit in with your life plan. You're hoping you'll never have to face that one."

We'd arrived at the biggest fairy tale of them all—love, marriage, and the prince on the white horse.

At the beginning of any relationship, the sexual attraction is so consuming that you believe that warm, tingly feeling deep inside will last forever. You don't want to listen to your friends when they warn you that the sexual intensity isn't going to last. You don't want your relationship to change; you like it just the way it has been. Besides, you believe that your relationship is different and more sexually charged than any other in the whole world, so it won't change.

Then you learn that indeed your friends were right. Sexual intensity *doesn't* last. Over time, it changes. It's not as passionate and consuming as it was at the start.

In the beginning of your relationship, you also ignore any telltale signs—and there are many—of little things your new partner does that annoy you. You put up with them because everything he does is cute. But they're not cute for long.

Things like flossing in front of you while you're trying to drink your coffee or read the newspaper. Or leaving his toothbrush on the counter in a tiny pool of water instead of shaking it dry and putting it back in the holder where it belongs.

In the beginning there are many things you overlook and think you can live with. But they become annoying when you have to deal with them day in and day out.

Then there are the larger issues that sometimes arise as you spend more time as a married couple. Maybe you discover that, even though you thought you knew your partner before you got married, you each have very different goals and dreams. Perhaps, as you grow older, you also grow apart. You start to wonder how the two of you have lost the connection you once had, and you wonder who this person really *is* who's sitting across from you at breakfast. It's then that you may start to question yourself and your ability to have a lasting, committed relationship.

"I don't look at my first two marriages as total failures," I tell my girls. "I've learned that experiences like these are the building blocks that make you who you are. Disappointments, setbacks, and even seemingly total failures can be the mortar that holds you together. You learn through a process. When bad things happen, you need to acknowledge the pain, deal with it, and—most important—*learn* from them. In time, you will understand the lessons you learned. And those lessons will build a stronger you.

"In reality, you—and only you—are responsible for yourself," I say. "Remember, too, that forgiveness sets you free."

I opened the second wedding album, and there I was standing beside a tall, dark, and handsome man, who I believed was Prince Charming personified.

"Speaking of forgiveness, I'm just going to cut to the chase," I tell my girls. "Enter Prince Dashing, John DeLorean. I met him at a charity function. On a bet."

—— ⚘ ——

John and another dashing friend of his were squiring women all over the world. It seems they had a pact: All the women who were over five feet, eight inches tall were John's, while the shorter ones went with his little buddy. He later told me that he bet his friend before he met me that I would be a tall one. Because I stand five feet, eight inches in my stocking feet, John won the bet. At the charity event, I walked over to the other side of the room and there I met my destiny.

John DeLorean, my second husband, was the stuff of which fairy tales are made. You couldn't help but notice him, and once you met him, you couldn't help being pulled in by his charisma. He was rich, powerful, and strikingly handsome with commanding green eyes. He stood six feet, five inches tall and was a self-made man. He was brilliant. His voice was velvety rich, and I loved to just listen to him speak. There was always a whirlwind of excitement around him. The moment we met, there was a clashing of cymbals.

John was the president of General Motors Truck and Cars Division for the United States and Canada. He cut a dashing figure in his designer suits, and had pursued and dated many beautiful women. I was flattered that he took an interest in me. I was twenty-four, at the pinnacle of my modeling career, and about to fall madly in love.

We married after a short courtship, and I was positive I was going to live the rest of my life with this man. I felt safe with him. He was extremely charismatic and quickly controlled any room he walked into. We made noise everywhere we went. We were constantly on the move with the press following behind us.

With John, I had an instant family. During his previous marriage, he had adopted Zachary, whom I adopted a year after our marriage. What more could I ask for? These two glorious people were going to be in my life. *How lucky could I get?*

The wedding was small, thirty people in all, including my immediate family. I wore a cream-colored sleek chiffon floor-length dress, belted in the middle. A tiny bouquet of flowers, lilacs and lily of the valley, pinned to the middle of my collar gave the dress a splash of color. My hair was pulled into a chignon and pinned in the back with the same arrangement of flowers. High-heeled, strapped satin sandals completed the simple look.

Before taking my fairy-tale walk down the aisle, I stared at myself in the mirror for a last-minute touchup. I stopped to look long and hard at my face. *This is it,* I thought. I was sure of it. I was going to live happily ever after. *How could it ever end?*

Now when I look back on those days so many years ago, I can finally be objective and see the marriage for what it really was and not what I pretended it to be. The relationship was built on superficiality, fluff, gloss, and unconditional love about as deep as a puddle.

I married for all the wrong reasons. This is tough to admit, even today. I totally bought into the power, the lifestyle, the shimmering lights, and what I thought was social acceptance.

It was all pretty heady. We were the darlings of New York, and I fell for all the trappings. We lived in a fourteen-room apartment on Fifth Avenue. On Fridays we would head to our five-hundred-acre estate in Bedminster, New Jersey. In the summers, we would go to the Hamptons to attend glamorous soirees with our "friends." We dined at the finest restaurants and were seated at their best tables. All of the top designers were making my clothes. Many would *give* me clothes to wear to important functions because they knew I would be photographed in them. Even as I'm writing this, I'm cringing at how shallow all of this sounds.

"Was I really that shallow?" I ask my girls beside the box of marriage memories.

"Like yeah, mom, you were. But don't stop talking now," they say. "Get it all out!"

John left General Motors to start his own automobile company, DeLorean Motor Company. Always the maverick, he set up his headquarters in New York instead of Detroit. Everyone watched and waited to see what would happen next.

Equally successful, I was modeling for the covers of all the leading magazines and enjoying a thriving career as a cover girl and commercial spokesperson. I was making a lot of money and was proud of the fact that I was able to take care of the things I needed for myself. It gave me satisfaction to know that I didn't have to go to John when I wanted something, and that I contributed to our income.

I was totally immersed in our fast-paced lifestyle, so it was easy to force myself to ignore a nagging doubt: I always felt that John married me on the rebound from his very beautiful second wife, model/actress Kelly Harmon. It hurt him deeply that the marriage to her didn't work out. He talked openly about how it devastated him.

I honestly believe that he was not in love with me when we married, and never loved me in the way a husband truly loves his wife. Of course I didn't realize any of this until my third marriage, to Tony, who showed me what true, unconditional love really is all about. So now I can say without hesitation that there was something seriously wrong with how John and I conducted ourselves as husband and wife.

I was so caught up in our busy make-believe "fairy tale" life that I didn't realize we never connected as true lovers, partners, or even friends. We never spoke to each other about our feelings or desires. We never had in-depth discussions on anything, really.

We shared two children, first Zachary and later our daughter, Kathryn. But we never really connected as a unit to raise them. He had one relationship with them, and I had another. We could never agree on how to discipline them, so I took over because he was on business trips most of the time.

I was crazy about the kids and loved being a mother. I planned play dates, birthday parties, and outings. John was always traveling or working very long hours. I never really missed him all that much because we didn't ever connect when he was home. I was fine with living in my beautiful homes with my great kids, because back then I couldn't see just how shallow my life was.

I was free to do my own thing. John didn't seem to care what I did. I continued to model and spend a lot of time in Los Angeles with the kids so I could be near my mom, dad, sister, and brother. Whenever I wanted to go anywhere with the kids, I would just pick up and leave. If John wanted to join us, fine. This went on for years. We were leading two separate lives, only coming together for show. Consequently, when it came time to cope with disaster, there was nothing to keep our fairy-tale world from falling apart.

———— ⚜ ————

The phone call came in the middle of a birthday party I had thrown for a friend. We were in my home in Manhattan.

"Please take a message," I said. But I was urged to take the call, even though I've always had a rule in my home: no phone calls during dinner. I got up, rather annoyed. *What could possibly be so important?* Talk about defining moments.

"Good evening, Mrs. DeLorean," said the voice. "My name is Bill, I'm from the *Los Angeles Times*, and I just wanted to get your reaction and any statement you might have regarding your husband's arrest."

His remarks didn't even register. He repeated what he just said. I stood there in a daze.

"Excuse me?" I asked. "What husband are you talking about? Not *my* husband! You must have the wrong person."

Irritated, I demanded, "Who *is* this?"

He introduced himself once more, and then told me that John had been arrested in a hotel room in downtown Los Angeles for allegedly buying and selling cocaine.

What in the world was he talking about? My husband was arrested for dealing what?

I told him he'd made a huge mistake. "It's someone else's husband you're talking about," I insisted.

I was in shock. My friend came over to ask me what was wrong. I couldn't even speak. She took the phone from my hand and asked what was happening. She was told the same thing. I thought it was a joke.

It was no joke.

That phone call changed the course of my life, my children's lives, and the lives of those who were closest to me.

I flew to L.A., completely unprepared for the abyss of lies and deceit that I was about to enter. As the events leading up to John's arrest started to unfold on national and international news, I was caught up in a nightmare.

The media attention was unrelenting. Every time I turned on the television, I was faced with the same clip of John sitting in a hotel room looking at an open suitcase filled with bags of cocaine, along with his instantly classic comment about how it was "better than gold." The tape of him being arrested and handcuffed was aired every single time they mentioned the arrest on the news. It was the biggest story at the time, so the arrest was mentioned in every newspaper and on every broadcast of every news program.

My thoughts immediately turned toward the children. *What if they saw their father in handcuffs, being carted off to jail?* It pained me deeply to see John treated this way. I felt desperate, but I remained duped. I still felt there had been a *huge* mistake. *This could not be happening!*

There is a story here, a monumental one. It has all the elements of a compelling page-turner. International intrigue involving two governments, F.B.I. informants, a sting operation, death threats, kidnapping threats, millions of dollars, money laundering, drugs, and the jet-set mentality that defined the latter part of the seventies and the eighties. That story will probably be told someday. But not by me.

I made a promise to myself that I would not publicly say anything negative about John because of the children. They had been hurt enough by what happened to our family. They didn't need to see in print their mother saying anything bad, damaging, demeaning, or hurtful about their dad, ever.

I will say this. In the beginning, I was fiercely loyal and protective. As the months leading up to his trial approached, however, I became increasingly aware that I really didn't have a clue as to who John really was. How could I? We never communicated with each other on a deep emotional level. We never shared intimate secrets, childhood stories, or feelings with one another.

It pains me to say this now, but I had absolutely no idea of John's financial woes, other than that the DeLorean Motor Company had its problems, just as most young companies do. But I wasn't involved in them, because John never shared his business life with me. We shared only the fairy tale, which smashed into a hundred thousand pieces.

Communication never broke down because there was never any to begin with. All I knew was that by the time the trial approached, two years after his arrest, I was living with a stranger. After almost eleven years, I was embarrassed to admit I never knew or understood him as a person.

I tried to hang on, thinking (unrealistically) that I could salvage our marriage. *We could start all over for the sake of the kids.* But it just didn't work out. He was emotionally detached. Who could blame him?

John seemed to relish the notoriety, the life in perpetual spin control. You can get a high off of that, I guess. But I couldn't understand it. We were all caught up in the drama of a very serious situation.

The trial lasted for five very long months. Thank God for Howard Weitzman. He is considered one of the finest criminal attorneys in the country, and he defended John. He was brilliant. I felt safe and reassured by his presence. One by one, Howard refuted each and every charge until there were none. In the end, John was acquitted on all counts and I was left with a lifelong friend in Howard who, to this day, I'm extremely close to and truly love.

During that long and arduous trial, our already feeble relationship was eroding, piece by piece. The stress I endured over that period left me exhausted, feeling like one big, raw, exposed nerve. When the jury foreperson stood up in the courtroom and read the verdict— "Not guilty—" I cried. No, I *convulsed*. I broke down and sobbed for nearly three hours straight. I couldn't stop. We couldn't leave the courthouse to go home because I had completely lost control of myself.

Reporters from all over the world had camped out in front of the Los Angeles Criminal Courts Building during this whole ordeal, and they waited anxiously for us to come out. I couldn't face the hordes of reporters, well-wishers, and angry mobs who were extremely vocal about his acquittal.

I realize now that I wasn't sobbing just because we had reached the end of this ordeal; I was mourning the loss of my marriage. I finally saw through the shallowness of my make-believe marriage and my make-believe life. I had forgotten who I was; I had lost myself when I fell for the fairy-tale marriage and the fairy-tale life, and it took me a while to remember reality. This breakdown was apparently the beginning of that process.

I stayed in California with my kids while John went back to New York to prepare for yet another ordeal. He had RICO charges—Racketeer Influenced and Corrupt Organization Act, very serious stuff— brought against him in Detroit, and he had to go there for yet another trial. Once again, Howard Weitzman defended him, and once again, John was acquitted. After that, I asked for a divorce.

———— ⚘ ————

The emptiness I had been feeling for so long quietly gave way to numbness, until I couldn't feel anything any more. All of our "friends" disappeared except for one, the best one—Eileen Burns, or "Auntie Leeny," as the girls call her. At first I was confused and devastated, then I was angry, and now I am finally grateful. I think when they coined the phrase "fair-weather friends," they had already met ours.

My immediate family stood by my kids and me without the slightest reservation. They lifted our spirits and showed us what unconditional love is truly all about. I settled into our new life and gathered my family close around me. I closed up my heart, just as I'd closed up the big apartment in Manhattan, and moved to L.A. with the children to be near my parents. *No more love, no more fairy tales, no more men, no more princes. . . .*

I was completely closed to the idea of getting seriously involved ever again. I was going to raise my two kids and date only ski instructors. At least, I thought, they're seasonal!

During my pregnancies, I felt like Jabba the Hut. Can I get any bigger?

CHAPTER 4

The Myth of a
Painless Childbirth

THE GIRLS ARE GIGGLING in unison, holding a photo of a bulbous me in maternity clothes, a snapshot from one of my pregnancies. It's the fairy tale that comes after love and marriage: the baby carriage.

Ever since I was a little girl, I wanted to be a mom. I became aware of that desire when I was about five. For Christmas that year, I was given a large box with a huge red bow, which I had been eyeing under our tree for over two weeks, eagerly anticipating the treasure awaiting inside.

Our family tradition was to open our presents *after* dinner on Christmas Eve. I hated that. It always took *so-o-o* long to eat. My sister, brother, cousins, and I wanted to tear open those boxes right away so we could play. But no, we had to eat first.

Around the holidays, our house would be filled with people and, of course, with food. All week, my mom and my aunts would prepare for the Christmas Eve feast. Our tradition was to eat fish, and not just any old fish. I'm talking about heaps of giant fresh shrimp, calamari, octopus, halibut, and trout.

We had so much food that my dad had to build my mom a second kitchen in our basement to prepare it all. Laughter and singing always rang from that second kitchen, where the heady smells of garlic, olive oil, and fresh herbs wafted up into the living room, creating an exciting anticipation leading up to that special night. The memory of those special smells and feelings has remained with me all these many years.

Finally, the Christmas Eve dinner hour would arrive, and we'd all sit at the long, food-laden table. We would start with the antipasto course. Large platters were piled with salami, prosciutto, mortadella, cheeses, olives, marinated peppers, roasted eggplant, baby artichokes, sautéed mushrooms, and, finally, freshly baked breads.

The antipasto was, of course, a meal in itself. Did we stop there? *Heavens no!* Next came the pasta course, followed by more pasta— linguine with calamari. Then the fish and vegetable course. We kids were so full after the antipasto that we became bored and agitated as we waited while the grownups ate, laughed, drank, and talked, endlessly. I couldn't understand why they were so slow, and why they weren't as excited as we kids were to push back from the table and get on with the opening of the gifts.

At long last, my mother would give the signal to move out of the dining room and over to the Christmas tree. Dad would dim the lights. Christmas music played in the background. As we kids raced into the living room, the tree would be glowing in front of the huge picture window, which framed it perfectly. You could see the snow falling sideways outside before it gently touched the ground. The streetlights reflecting on the snow gave the impression of diamonds sparkling.

But all I could see on the day I'm remembering now is that big box with the red bow.

I ran directly to it. I tore it open, wondering what new and wondrous places this new toy was going to take me. As I lifted the lid and pushed apart the delicate tissue, I saw my future lying there.

My first baby doll!

Not just any baby doll. This was a Tiny Tears doll. She was the size of a newborn baby and had a head full of teeny tiny strands of curly brown hair. Her skin was soft, just like a real infant's. She had dimpled hands and feet, chubby little thighs, and a tiny belly. She was brand-new on the market, and on every little girl's wish list. Tiny Tears was different from any other doll. She drank *real* juice from a bottle, and, best of all, she would pee, so you had to change her diaper for real!

I fell in love with her immediately. I named her Tiny, and she was my baby.

My maternal instincts kicked in early. From the moment I opened that box and saw Tiny, I was obsessed with babies. It didn't matter whose baby it was: my baby sister, my baby brother, my neighbor's babies, babies on the street. I wanted to take care of them all. I couldn't wait to get married so I could have *nine* babies of my own!

Flash-forward a couple of decades, to reality.

—— ✿ ——

My first marriage was to a man named Nick. I was nineteen, and wanted to have a baby *immediately*. My fairy tale of the baby carriage didn't include the notion that I might have trouble conceiving.

But month after month rolled by, and I never missed a period. I was heartbroken each time my period came—a reminder that, yet again, I was not pregnant. My feelings turned into devastation, then desperation.

Later, when I married John DeLorean, he was already in the process of adopting Zachary, a fourteen-month-old baby boy. I became Zachary's legal mother after I went through the adoption procedures. We were a cozy little family, and "Z" was the center of our lives; but we kept trying to have another child.

After about two years of trying to no avail, I decided to seek medical attention. First, we tested John to see if his sperm were viable. His count was low, but not so low that we couldn't conceive.

I was tested next. I had to go through a battery of tests to see if I was ovulating normally. They drew blood, and I had to pee into dozens of cups. They poked and prodded, sticking things in me that looked more like weapons of torture than medical devices. I even had dye injected into my fallopian tubes to see if they were clear.

All systems were go, and the doctor explained that there is a window of opportunity for a few days in the middle of your cycle when you are able to conceive. An elevation in temperature can indicate when this window might be. I was instructed to start using a temperature chart. I had to take my temperature every morning at the same time for three months. This was so we could pinpoint *exactly* when I was ovulating.

As I added data to my chart, I found out exactly when I was most likely to conceive. Thus John and I began our "Sex on Demand" routine. It was awful, so unromantic. I felt like a robot. To make matters worse, when we were finished, I had to lie in bed for forty-five minutes with my legs in the air and a pillow under my ass! Humiliating wasn't the word. I just kept saying to myself that it was all worth it because, "We're going to have a baby!" However, I couldn't avoid the nagging thought that this was *not* the way it's supposed to happen.

If I was a day late, I was convinced I was pregnant. When my period started, as it inevitably would, I pretended it wasn't really happening. I would rush to bed, thinking if I got off my feet, the bleeding would stop. I was disappointed to the point of tears every time. *Oh well, there's always next month.*

After months and months of this "chart thing" with no results, I consulted a fertility specialist. He took me on a completely different journey, one of emotional highs and lows, not to mention multiple personalities.

I'm talking about fertility drugs.

Almost instantly, I gained twenty pounds. I was round, puffy, and extremely irritable. I felt horrible, and I hated everyone in the entire world. The drugs altered my personality to the point where *I* couldn't even stand to be with me. I stayed on fertility drugs for about six months. *Nothing, absolutely nothing.* After that, I just couldn't take it any longer. After a lot of soul-searching and tears, I decided to quit. I tried to accept the fact that I was one of those women who would never know the joy of childbirth. I had Zach, and in him I found a great deal of solace, comfort, and joy.

I was able to move on with my life, in spite of the pain I always felt at the sight of all the baby carriages in Central Park. After a while, I buried those feelings so deep that they couldn't hurt me anymore. When Zach was six, he started first grade. I walked him to school every day. I started to feel a dull ache in my lower abdomen during our walks, but I brushed it off as PMS. *It's about time, because I'm ten days late.* I had been late many times before, so this was nothing new. Since I was due for my annual checkup, I made an appointment for the following week. The odd pulling persisted, but I still thought nothing of it.

I had my physical, left a urine sample, and went home. The next day, the nurse called.

"Cristina, the doctor would like to speak to you," she said.

Uh-oh. Something is wrong. He's never asked to speak to me before.

I took a deep breath and waited.

"Well, you did it, sweetheart!" he exclaimed. "You're pregnant."

I didn't even ask him to repeat it because if he did, I was afraid he would take those words back. Or worse yet, tell me he read someone else's results by mistake. So I remained silent. I had waited for those words my whole life. I wanted to hold onto that moment forever.

"I know you don't believe this," he said. "But it's true. I want you in my office first thing in the morning so we can plan your pregnancy."

I hung up the phone and made a beeline for John and told him the news. We screamed like little kids in a schoolyard as we cried and jumped up and down! I called my mother and father and, still screaming, tried to tell them the news. My mother got hysterical because she thought someone was dead! I was so excited that she couldn't make out what I was saying.

"Mom, listen to me, I'M PREGNANT!" I screamed with hysterical delight, and I could hear screaming on her end, too.

I called every person I knew, and then every person I even remotely knew. The thrill of that moment will never leave me. I was 27, and I remember the day as if it were yesterday.

It's been 27 years since that life-altering moment. Since then, I have experienced the highest highs and the lowest lows as a parent. People can talk about what it's like to be pregnant and to raise a child, but you can *never* be prepared for the reality of what that experience is really all about.

I *immediately* rushed to the maternity store to buy clothes. I was only three weeks pregnant, but I was sure I was showing already. I bought pants with an elastic waist and a "maternity panel" in the front. *What a great excuse to eat! My pants will just expand with me!* I bought the basics to get me through and planned to purchase different tops as I grew.

My God, those clothes were ugly!

In those days, no one was designing stylish maternity clothes with materials that actually breathed. Pregnant women weren't expected to be stylish. Unlike today, if you would have walked outside then with a crop top and low-riding pants, exposing your stomach, someone would have come up to you to offer you their coat. I love the celebrities who boldly expose their pregnant bellies these days. Of course, they're the ones who don't have cellulite on their thighs, stretch marks on their bellies, and arms that flap in the wind.

My body changed rapidly. Right away, my breasts swelled two full cup sizes. Normally, one might be thrilled by this development, but they hurt and were extremely sensitive, especially around the nipples.

Great. How am I going to breastfeed if my breasts are too painful to even touch?

My doctor told me that the pulling I'd felt in my lower abdomen was the first clue to my pregnancy—my uterus was expanding. That pulling feeling lasted the whole nine months. But I was extremely lucky that I didn't experience serious morning sickness. I was only a bit queasy for the first three months.

In the beginning, I remember feeling extremely tired. I wanted to sleep all the time. On the rare occasions that I would actually nap, I found it very difficult to get up again. When I awoke, I'd be in a stupor, and it took some time for me to feel fully awake. I would pry open my eyes, prop myself up on one elbow, and try to focus. But I was so groggy! I actually had to work to remember what day it was. I found myself looking around the room and wondering where I was.

I never knew that human skin could actually stretch so far and not tear. By the time I was six months along, I looked like a Big Mac. I believe that six months is an appropriate amount of time to be pregnant, and anything beyond that is just not fair. Up until six months, you can still walk and not look like a penguin. Your tummy is firm and round and the size of a basketball. You're able to get into decent-looking shoes because you don't yet have swollen ankles and sausage toes. That mysterious brown line that starts at your pubic bone and ends at your belly button hasn't appeared yet, and your belly button doesn't stick out. When it finally pops out—and, believe me, it will—

you won't be able to hide it with clothes. You'll look like a Butterball turkey whose gauge is telling you, "Okay, I'm cooked! Time to come out of the oven!"

But your baby isn't a Butterball turkey, and it's still three months away from being ready. At six months, you're nowhere close to giving birth. You'll stay like that for many more weeks. Every time you turn sideways to catch a reflection of yourself in the mirror, you'll find yourself asking God, "Is this a joke?"

At the time of my first pregnancy, our bathroom had mirrors all over the walls. When I sat down to use the facilities, I would stare at myself in horror and cry because I looked like Jabba the Hut!

In my eighth month, my girlfriends decided to give me a baby shower. I was thrilled. It's exactly what's supposed to happen. You get together with a bunch of your dearest family and friends and have a luncheon, complete with flowers and a cake that's shaped like a baby buggy. You open presents for hours, and everyone coos, *"A-a-a-a-a-w-w-w!"* every time you hold up a tiny new outfit. Forget the fact that you can't dress an infant in any of these. Your baby will stay in Carters T-shirts with snaps and those pajamas with the feet for three months. It's just easier, and you'll want "easy" once the baby is born.

After all, real babies don't just pee like the Tiny Tears doll. Real babies spit up and need changing so often that it's not convenient to put them in fancy outfits. By the time they're ready to be in those outfits, they've outgrown them. So you wrap up the outfits ever so carefully, putting them away with every intention of giving them to your child when he or she has a baby.

I have all of those baby clothes waiting somewhere in my closets, or moving boxes, now.

During my pregnancy, I went from 125 to 185 pounds. I used my pregnancy as an excuse to eat, which was a big mistake. I jeopardized my health by gaining so much weight and ended up developing a form of diabetes caused by excessive weight gain. This was never mentioned in the pregnancy books I diligently read.

By the ninth month, my doctor said that I could no longer have intercourse or take hot baths. "We don't want to disturb anything and give birth too early," he cautioned.

Too early? I was ready to explode, but by now I was scared to give birth. *How in the world is something that size going to come out of me?*

No matter how much you read or how many birthing classes you go to, you can never be prepared for childbirth. It happened to me for the first time at 3:30 A.M. on November 15, 1977. I was awakened with a jolt, and when I came out of my stupor, I discovered that I was soaking wet. At first I thought I'd wet the bed. From the time I learned I was expecting, I had to go to the bathroom three or four times a night, sometimes for just a trickle. The pressure on my bladder always felt like I was going to explode. So I just thought I hadn't awakened in time.

"Help me up," I said as I nudged John. During my last month, he literally had to help me out of bed. It was like moving a beached whale. I couldn't get out unless he rolled me over on my side and then lifted me to a sitting position. Forget about seeing my feet! I just navigated until I felt the floor, then stood up.

"I wet the bed," I said on that fateful November morning.

"Charming," was his reply. "Maybe your water just broke."

"Oh my God, of course!" I said. "My water broke!"

I wanted to call the doctor, but I was embarrassed to phone him at such an ungodly hour. Besides, our Lamaze instructor told us over and over, "After your water breaks, you can expect twelve to fourteen hours of labor. The baby won't come right away."

But I decided to call the doctor anyway because I was just plain scared. He was so calming as he told me to meet him at the hospital.

Another thing I didn't expect when I was growing up believing in fairy tales: having to hail a New York City cab in winter at 4:00 A.M. while having contractions.

Every time I took a step, I would leak. Water just kept coming out.

"Just stay still, and I'll hail the cab," John told me.

After about twenty minutes standing in the cold, I felt my first contraction. I started to panic. But then John's frantic waving caused a Yellow Cab to slow to a stop. In a gushing of verbiage, we both told the cabbie what was going on. He was very sweet, but he proceeded to tell us horror stories of taking pregnant women to the hospital. "I actually helped deliver a baby with some help from the cops," he said. "So not to worry."

Oh, great, I thought.

The guy hit every pothole. And believe me, I felt each jolt.

Finally, we arrived at the hospital. In those days, they didn't have pre-registration, so I had to sit in the general waiting room until someone led me to a smaller waiting room. The contractions were coming about twenty minutes apart. Every time that happened, more water leaked out. The pain was manageable, and I started thinking that this was going to be a piece of cake. Then I started to wish I had some cake.

I was finally taken to a tiny cubicle, where the attendant actually asked me, "What are you in for?"

That did it.

"It's almost Halloween, and I'm masquerading as a building!" I said.

John grabbed my hand and squeezed it; he knew my responses weren't going to be in a civil tone. "My wife is in her ninth month, and she's having contractions," he said.

I was ready to be brought to the birthing room. The attendant wanted to relive the Spanish Inquisition. The questions went on for days. "What happens to women who come in here with contractions three minutes apart?" I finally asked my inquisitor.

"We don't admit anyone without making sure we have all of your information and insurance," she replied.

Okay, fine. Here's my insurance. NOW GET ME IN A ROOM!

Not yet. She also needed John's insurance, plus any secondary insurance. It took almost an hour and fifteen minutes to register. After someone put my nametags around my wrists, the attendant asked me seventeen times if I was the person on the tag.

"Excuse me, have we not been here the whole time together?" I asked incredulously. "Was someone else in and out of this room while I was giving you my life story?"

John just tried to keep me calm.

They put me in another room, where I waited for some guy who came in with a wheelchair to finally take me to the maternity ward. He wheeled me onto the elevator that would deliver me to the floor where I would spend the next seven days. Yes, I said *seven* days. As the doors slid open, I was relieved to know that soon I'd be in a room where I could feel safe. I was filled with excitement and anxiety, fear and trepidation.

As I was wheeled down the corridor to my room, I could hear other women groaning, some louder than others. I was really nervous, but I didn't have long to dwell on anything. Because soon a friendly face with a beautiful calming smile greeted me. "I'm your nurse," she said, introducing herself. She immediately made me feel comfortable and explained everything that I could expect.

Everything except for what would actually happen!

She strapped a fetal monitor onto my belly, and we could hear the baby's heartbeat. It was beating so fast that I got concerned there might be something wrong. But my nurse reassured me that the heartbeat was perfectly normal. "That's just what it sounds like," she said, walking out the door. "You're fine. I'll check in on you later."

At different intervals, different doctors stopped by to check on how I was doing. They snapped on those elastic gloves and stuck their fingers up *there* to see how many centimeters I was dilated. "Two," one doctor told me, then another and another. I'd been two centimeters for the last three doctors. How I wished I had paid better attention in math class. They say when you're ten centimeters, you can push. *How wide is that?*

Another doctor came by and asked, "Did you lose your mucus plug?"

Excuse me? I don't know you. Why am I going to discuss the loss of my mucus plug with you?

I very politely expressed my thanks for his concern over my plug, but added, "I don't feel comfortable discussing it with you." *Who are these people anyway, and where is my real doctor?*

It seems that I had landed in a teaching hospital, and all these doctors coming in and out of my room were just students using me as a guinea pig. I put a stop to that and refused to open my legs for anyone until I could see my own doctor.

He finally arrived around 8:30.

I was so mad at him! How dare he not be at the hospital when I arrived? But I didn't want to tell him that I was mad because I was also really nervous, and I didn't want him to be angry with me. He checked me out and announced, "Cristina, you're two centimeters dilated!" *Great! I could have told him that!*

"This will take a while," he said.

"How long is a while?" I asked anxiously.

"Oh, about six to eight hours," he said as he checked his watch. *Six to eight hours. Oh my God, kill me NOW!*

The doctor said he was going to his office but would check on my progress with the nurse, and would return when my contractions were three minutes apart. I couldn't believe he was going to leave. The nurse assured me that everything would be fine, and she would be there to make sure.

My contractions came every fifteen minutes for about five hours, and then they just stopped. By then, my armada of visiting physicians told me that I was four centimeters dilated. But nothing was happening! The nurse kept checking the heart monitor, and I didn't like the way she was looking at it.

"What's wrong?" I asked.

"Nothing yet," she said. "But I'm going to call the doctor."

When he arrived, he said, "We're going to prep you for a C-section. Your water broke over twelve hours ago and you're not progressing. It's putting stress on the baby."

Before I had a chance to respond, nine people were in my room. They stuck more needles into my arm, and began shaving my stomach and pubic area. They painted my whole stomach, using a paintbrush with yellow iodine. I looked like an igloo that an elephant peed on! They also stuck a pen in my hand, because I had to sign more forms in case I died in the operating room.

I looked over to John, but he was no help. By then, he had turned *green.* He opted not to go into the operating room.

My crew rolled me down the hall, fast. I kept wishing that my mom were there with me, but she was in L.A. So I just stared at the ceiling and watched the lights overhead whiz by. It was surreal.

Just like in the movies, I could hear the operating room doors opening with a "Voom!" I was wheeled into a cold, sterile room that felt like a meat locker. I started shivering immediately, as all of the activity swirled around me.

This is it? This is what I have been waiting for all my life?

I was scared . . . cold . . . convinced there was something wrong with my baby.

Where's my husband? Isn't he supposed to be here by my side telling me to focus and take a deep, cleansing breath? Why did I spend all those hours in Lamaze class? They only concentrated on natural childbirth. They never discussed C-sections!

The doctor told me that he was going to give me general anesthesia.

Just put me out so I don't feel cold or scared or . . . anything!

As anesthesia entered my arm, I could feel a burning sensation in my hand. They placed a mask over my mouth. Meanwhile, I tried to focus on positive thoughts: *I'll fall asleep, and when I awake, I'll have a baby! Piece of cake.*

I woke up to a woman's voice that kept repeating my name. *Shut up!* I thought. *Leave me alone.* As I started to rally, the voice said, "You've given birth to a baby girl." I had a millimeter of a second where I felt joy beyond compare. But then I started to move and felt a searing pain in my abdomen.

Wow! No one told me it was going to hurt this much!

I slept most of the next twenty-four hours. When I awoke, Nurse From Hell was standing over me. "Okay, get up," she snapped, without introduction. "Time to go for our walk."

Our walk? Is she insane? I can hardly breathe without pain; how does she expect me to walk?

I protested, but she wouldn't listen. Nurse From Hell insisted, and she wasn't going to leave until I complied. "You gotta walk to avoid blood clots," she said, tugging at my arm.

I couldn't believe how much it hurt to move. It took twenty minutes for me to place my feet on the ground. When I finally stood up and put the weight of my entire body on my feet, I almost hurled from the searing pain.

"Okay, so now I'm standing," I said. "Where do you want me to go?"

"We're going to take a walk down to the nursery so you can see your baby," she announced in a military voice.

That was an incentive! I realized for the first time that I hadn't yet seen my baby girl. I'd been in such a stupor of pain that I hadn't even thought beyond myself. I adjusted my hair a bit and tried to close the back of the hospital gown that kept flapping open. But just lifting my arms was a painful ordeal. Everything hurt—breathing, talking, walking. Forget about even coughing. I never realized how you use your abdominal muscles to do everything.

Nurse From Hell gave me my IV stand to hang onto, and with the bottle on a rack rolling behind us, we began our journey down the hall to the nursery. I looked like Tim Conway doing his little old man routine. You know, the one where it takes him ten minutes to move two feet? *At least I get to see my baby*, I keep thinking, and that thought pushed me forward in spite of the pain.

When I arrived at the huge glass window outside the nursery, I could see all the beautiful babies wrapped in their blue or pink blankets. I eyed all the pink ones, and looked for our name. Nurse From Hell, in her single act of random kindness, pointed out my baby to me.

That moment became seared in my heart forever. The feeling of love, motherhood, and much more, was instant and consuming. I couldn't believe my eyes. I insisted that as soon as I got back to my room, I wanted to hold her.

"No," Nurse From Hell said. "We'll have to make sure you're fully awake and able to hold the baby without trouble before we let you hold her."

When I finally got back to my bed, I waited an eternity for them to bring her to me. To make the moment extra special, John had just arrived, and he wheeled her in to me. He gently reached into the bassinet and picked her up. She seemed so small, and as he handed her to me, I started to cry. Everything I ever dreamed of was handed to me that very moment. Everything else that had happened before didn't matter. As I held her, the pain in my body didn't even matter. The moment I held her in my arms, everything just went away.

John just looked at the two of us and was overwhelmed. He asked me if we could name her after his mother.

So we named her Kathryn.

Tony and I on our wedding day.
This photo personifies our relationship—joy and laughter
and the freedom to be ourselves.

CHAPTER 5

Remarriage and the Brady Bunch Syndrome

THE GIRLS RESCUE ANOTHER STACK of rubber-banded photos from the depths of a packing crate. Arianna picks off one photo from the top of the stack.

"Oh, look, it's you and Daddy on your wedding day!" she says.

"How did you meet him?" asks Alexandra.

"Was it love at first sight?" echoes Arianna.

No, I say, it was something closer to hate at first sight.

"I thought he was a corporate, stuck-up, arrogant jerk," I confess. "That's probably because he didn't give me the time of day."

When Tony and I met for the first time in 1979, I was still married to John DeLorean. Tony was the chairman of ABC television. I went up to his office to meet with him in hopes of landing an anchoring job on *Good Morning America*. The meeting was short and to the point. He kept me waiting forty-five minutes, didn't apologize for being late, and had a big-shot corporate attitude that didn't sit well with me. I thought he was a giant ass and left there wondering why I had even wasted my time. When I didn't get the job, I thought he was an even bigger ass.

I went about my life and would occasionally run into "Mr. Thomopoulos" at different functions around Los Angeles and New York. He was really handsome, but I still thought he was a jerk. Maybe that was because he never paid any attention to me. Not that I was looking for any—I was married and so was he. But I would have appreciated some kind of acknowledgment that he recognized me; he never offered it. No "Hello," no "How are you?" not even a "You have spinach in your teeth." *Nothing!* Why did it bother me so?

When I look back at that time so many years ago, I realize that it was fate that brought me up to meet with Tony in his office for the first time. I believe we were meant to be together, but first I had to travel through a nightmare in order to recognize unconditional love and my true soul mate.

When Tony and I finally got together, it was in the midst of a most unsettling time for both of us. He had been divorced for two years. John's trial was finally over, but we were still reeling from its residual effects. We had separated.

I rented a house in Los Angeles near my parents and told the kids only that, "Daddy has to stay in New York for a while." I never thought that they wouldn't accept this brand-new life. Naïve, you say? I probably was. After enduring months of stress during the trial, I was just happy to get my life back on track again. I looked forward to the prospect of giving my kids a normal existence.

Once I had time to settle into my new life, I was ready to face the world again. I slowly started to incorporate new people into our lives. One of them was Tony Thomopoulos.

I ran into Tony again at a mutual friend's birthday party. It was a black-tie affair. I was alone, and he had a date. At one point in the evening, I found myself sitting all alone at the table. Everyone was up dancing. Tony happened to catch my eye. When he came closer to say hello, I simply asked him if he would like to dance. He hesitated and then very politely said, "No." I felt the blood rushing to my ears. I'm sure I was the color of Georgia clay! I was so humiliated. What an ass!

He turned to leave, but then he slowly turned back around, held out his hand, and said, "You know what? I would love to dance with you." I was still too much in shock from the rejection to react, so I simply got up like a zombie and followed him to the dance floor. He put his arm around my waist and pulled me in to him. I caught a whiff of his cologne, and that was it.

I don't remember the music. I don't remember the conversation. I don't even remember the dance. All I know is that once that dance was over, I knew that I was in trouble. No more ski instructors for me. When Tony asked if he could call me, I gave him every number I had, including my mother's, just in case he misplaced mine.

We started seeing each other quietly. We fell hard and fast, and we knew from our first date that we were going to be married.

Once we did make a connection, which was on our first date—*Whatever happened to my resolve?*—it was all over. Instinctively, I *knew* this was going to be the person with whom I would spend the rest of my life. There was simply no turning back. The moment he touched me, I felt my body blend into his as the two of us became one.

When we kissed for the first time, I thought I was going to die. Everything about him felt so right. His kiss, the way he loved me, and the way he made love to me made me feel like I never had before. Intoxicating is the only way I can describe it. I had never experienced this kind of raw emotion rolled up in one dynamic man.

Tony and I were dizzy with love. The world was beautiful as long as we were together. We could walk through Central Park in winter without a jacket and still be warm. We would sit for hours and talk, or we would read for long periods of time without uttering a single word.

We ended each other's sentences and were extremely sensitive to each other's needs. Our passion for one another was insatiable. Every time he entered a room, my heart would skip a beat. He would call me in the middle of the day just to tell me that when I wasn't with him, he found it difficult to breathe. I realize this sounds dopey, but our emotions were so deep and strong that we couldn't imagine being without each other.

Despite the heady emotions we were feeling, we were careful to build our marriage on fundamentals, not fairy tales. Both of us shared a passion for family, a strong work ethic, and a focus on spirituality. We put these first, and our relationship grew and thrived.

When the minister said "For better or for worse," I really, truly thought, *With this wonderful man by my side, I can get through anything!* Those words are so easy when you're standing at the altar in the glow of a new marriage, and the "better" is so great and the "worse" is inconceivable.

But the "worse" always happens, and when it happens to one of you, it happens to *both* of you.

—— ⁂ ——

When we married, Tony was president of the ABC Television Broadcast Group. He was a major player in the entertainment industry, in a very powerful position. Three months into our marriage, Capital Cities Industries acquired ABC and his job was history. *Gone.* After a thirteen-year career at ABC, he was told that his services were no longer required. *Thank you, and goodbye.* It was a major adjustment for him, to say the least. He was facing his future and questioning his long-term ability to provide for his family. He couldn't concentrate on me and our relationship; he had to figure out what he was going to do with the rest of his life. I needed to stop thinking of myself and become his partner.

This time, the "worse" happened to Tony; next time, it might happen to me. It was my turn to be the loving, supportive partner.

So our life took a turn. It's nothing that can't be fixed. This was an unforeseen circumstance. Things change. As a couple, you go through good times, rough times, and changing times. Change turned out to be good, believe it or not.

Not too long after being ousted at ABC, Tony was asked to be the chairman of United Artists Pictures, a major motion picture studio. He was instrumental in bringing the Oscar-winning movie *Rain Man* to the screen. When he left United Artists, he went to Amblin Entertainment, the company owned by director Steven Spielberg on the Universal Studios lot. While at Amblin, he came across an old script that was sitting in the archives at Warner Brothers Studios. He read it, loved it, and thought it would make a terrific television series. It went on the air on NBC in 1995. Its name was *ER*. It has never left the top ten.

I have learned many lessons from Tony. This was an early and important one: Change can be good. I learned that when things get shaky and you're afraid of change, you need to talk it over with one another and express your fears and concerns instead of bottling them up inside. If you don't express your feelings, they're sure to manifest themselves in ugly behavior, resentment, and other damaging thoughts and actions.

This time I made sure to communicate with my partner on a daily basis. We talked about our feelings on everything from losing a job to what colors we don't like. The minute something came up, we talked about it. Somehow when you get the problem out in the open, it loses its punch—no matter how big it is!

It's when you *stop* talking, when you stop trying to work things out, that trouble starts. The minute a situation becomes uncomfortable, most people don't want to talk about it; they just want to flee. I've learned that if you can work through these rough spots, you can emerge on the other side, where you'll be stronger as a couple and, oddly enough, closer and more committed to one another. There's no question that you'll experience countless ups and downs as a couple. It's how you handle them that will determine the outcome of your commitment.

The most important ingredient in our marriage is our spirituality and commitment to God. That is what has kept us strong in good, bad, and devastating times. It's what has made the most significant difference in our marriage. We pray together as a couple and go to church as a family because it strengthens us and keeps us grounded.

Tony is my best friend in the whole world. I can't imagine life without him. We fight hard, work hard, play hard, and love hard. After almost twenty years together, we've been through quite a few devastating circumstances, but we've always come out of them stronger and more committed to each other.

Over the years, the intensity of our commitment has deepened. I'm not even sure where that comes from. It just happens. We are bonded together and we know it. Can this bond be broken? Yes, it can, but the real question is *"Will* it be broken?" *Will I work to keep us together, even in the roughest spots?* Absolutely.

That resolve was put to a very big test early on in our relationship, as we struggled to blend our families into one.

——— ⚘ ———

When Tony and I married, my children from my second marriage inherited one stepsister and two stepbrothers, all then teenagers. Tony's kids—Anne, Denis, and Mark—had gone through the rigors of puberty only to be faced with a new stepmother and two out-of-control teenage stepsiblings, Kathryn and Zach. Being an eternal optimist, I believed I could bring these two families together without a problem.

Will I ever learn? I must have watched too many episodes of *The Brady Bunch,* because that was how I really thought everything would turn out. The story I envisioned goes like this: A woman with two un-believably well-adjusted kids—despite a not-so-nice divorce—meets an incredibly handsome guy. After one date, they decide to marry. He has three great kids from a previous marriage. Her kids, upon hearing the news that this terrific guy will be their new stepfather, naturally are delighted. When told about his three kids, they are unable to be-lieve their great fortune. Even though they don't have enough room in their home for everyone, who cares? The kids will share their rooms, borrow each other's clothes, help with homework, and hang out with one another on the weekends. After all, they're looking for-ward to having a family unit again!

To make matters even more wonderful, the happy couple will get along *famously* with their exes, making the holidays so much easier when they all get together. Joy upon joy! They know it won't be all roses, but with patience, understanding, and a housekeeper who loves to pick up everything, they can make it work.

Call me naïve, but I honestly believed that when Tony and I mar-ried, his children would be crazy about me. Furthermore, there was no question in my mind that my children would absolutely love and accept their new stepdad. *How could they not?* I really thought they would see and love all the wonderful qualities he possessed that made me so happy.

From the moment we started dating, I was so insane for this man that I loved everything about him, including his children, whom I hadn't even met. It didn't matter. I loved everything in his life, in-cluding his penchant for beige. He was my Prince Charming, my knight in shining armor who would rescue me from all things "not nice."

We would discuss plans that included our children and what our lives would be like after we blended our families. What fun our vacations would be! We talked about the holidays and combining our Italian and Greek heritages to include everyone. How wonderful to have a big family to bring together for dinner, especially on Sundays!

I couldn't wait for him to meet my kids and my whole family. I just knew that when Tony and the kids met, they would really like one another. Perhaps we could plan to go to the beach or dinner and a movie. Perhaps they would embrace one another and get along so swimmingly that they would say, "Hey, I can't wait to start this new family together and make this thing work for us!"

Perhaps not. Once again, reality intervened, bursting my bubble.

—— ⚹ ——

When Tony met my daughter Kathryn, she was six years old. He and I arranged to "accidentally" meet on the street, and I would have Kathryn with me. I carefully combed her silky, blue-black hair into two perfect pigtails and tied the ends with red silk ribbons. I dressed her in her cutest outfit, and she looked adorable. I was so proud. She held my hand and skipped along, her pigtails flip-flopping in perfect cadence with her tiny jumps.

I could see Tony approaching from the other end of the block. The moment I saw him, my heart began pounding with anticipation. My thoughts started racing. *What would they say to one another?* I imagined Tony bending down and greeting her with his warm smile and a big hug. They would have a nice exchange, and later Kathryn would ask me about the "nice man" she had met that day, and tell me she hopes she will meet him again soon.

Of course, I had taught her how to practice good manners when she was introduced to people: how to be polite, look the person in the eye, shake hands, and say, "How do you do?" How could everything *not* be perfect?

As Tony approached, I slowed down our pace. When we were finally face-to-face, I greeted him with a hug and a peck on the cheek and told him how wonderful it was to run into him. With that, I started to introduce him to Kathryn.

She didn't wait for the introduction. She took one step forward and gave him a quick kick in the shins. I can still hear the *thwap!* as the steely tip of her shoe met with Tony's shin. Still holding my hand, she pulled me away, tugging me down the street, leaving Tony standing there, wincing in pain.

Oh, my Lord! I was horrified. Kathryn had never, ever done anything remotely like that in her life. Tony was as shocked as I was, and the incident set the tone for their relationship for many years to come. I stopped her, walked back to Tony, and immediately apologized. I demanded that Kathryn apologize as well.

"I'm sorry," she snapped in a tone that made it obvious she didn't mean it. We parted, and I took her home. Tony called fifteen minutes later. Needless to say, he thought Kathryn was a nasty child and simply didn't like her at all. "I got a very bad vibe from her," he said.

"A bad vibe?" I repeated. "She's six years old, for goodness sake! How can you make such a judgment from just one little kick?"

I was defensive because I felt very protective of her. How could he not like my child? We had our first fight—one of many—over the kids, and we weren't even married yet.

Although I felt protective of Kathryn, I didn't excuse her behavior. What she did was *way* out of line.

"Why would you do such a thing?" I asked her.

"Because I didn't like him," was all she said.

"That's not a reason to kick someone!" I said. "It's wrong, and I'm terribly disappointed." I grounded her for her behavior, and Kathryn blamed Tony. Now was not the time to tell her about our relationship.

My son Zach was easier. I had introduced him to Tony at some event, and Zach thought he was okay, cool, nice. He had no issues until, he said, Tony started to spend "too much time at our house."

"Mom," he would say, "why is this guy Tony spending so much time with us? You're not getting involved with him, are you?"

I realized with some annoyance that I would have to explain to my preteen son that "I'm an adult and I can see anyone I like." I also realized that I needed to keep myself in check and do this slowly. The pain in my heart was so heavy because I couldn't share my happy secret, plus I was acutely aware of how much my kids were still hurting from everything that had happened between their father and me.

As time went on, I realized that in order to move forward, I needed to be honest with my kids. Their father and I were going to get a divorce. When I walked into my kids' room to tell them the news, I was so sure that they would see this was the right move for us. After all, they had been living for quite a few years under the strain of two parents who were truly unhappy. Were they not witnesses to our arguing and all the tears? Did they not experience the frustration firsthand? How could they not know how miserable the situation was? They were living with it every day.

The memory of the moment when I told them that their father and I were divorcing will never leave me, and I'm sure it's forever burned into their memories as well. I asked Kathryn and Zach to sit down with me on the floor, thinking if we made a circle it would seem cozy and nonthreatening. Slowly and patiently, I began to explain how much both their father and I loved them and how we would always be there for them. "But the three of us are going to be making a new life for ourselves in California without Daddy, so we can be closer to my family," I said.

I waited for a reaction. But there was none. From the look on their faces, I realized they had no idea that this was coming. Then, they got angry.

"How dare you ruin our lives!" they both screamed in unison. "How can you be so selfish? What about Dad? Who's going to take care of Dad?"

They followed up this outburst, practically in the same breath, with, "You better not even think about dating or marrying anyone, *ever!* No matter who he is, we'll hate him and never ever accept him. And if he has kids, we'll hate them, too! We're not sharing a bedroom or a bathroom or a house with anyone!"

Do I ground them for using this tone of voice? Do I just let them get it all out? I was so traumatized by their reaction that for a split second, I actually thought about going back to their father. But they brought me back home when they proceeded to tell me how much they hated me and how much they wanted to go live with their father instead.

Whoa! Where did that come from? I guessed that this was *not* the time to tell them about Tony.

I felt trapped. I felt guilty and confused. *Was I making the right decision? Should I go back to John for the sake of the kids? How do I tell Tony that I can't be with him?*

You never really know how a moment like that will affect the rest of your kids' lives. It wasn't until after they were grown and we had conversations about that night that I started to understand exactly what they had gone through. I didn't come from a broken home, so I didn't have a point of reference. They told me how frightened, resentful, angry, and confused they had been. Anger was the emotion that topped their lists. Their anger was directed at me because I was the one who had interrupted their lives. They felt responsible for their father because I was the one who left the marriage.

They had always wished that their parents had stayed together.

Even now that they're grown, they still hold that wish deep down inside. Having to accept a new "Dad," step or not, had been really difficult for them. Their loyalty to their father far outweighed anything Tony could have done for them.

Overwhelmed by all of the emotions of the time, I chose not to deal with the psychological toll the divorce had taken on them. I pretended everything was going to be just fine. It wasn't.

When we all sat down as a family before Tony and I were married, I remember announcing to everyone, "I'm *so-o-o-o-o-o* happy! We'll be just like *The Brady Bunch*."

Thank goodness we can laugh about it now. But both sides of my family have reminded me of that comment more than once. I'll never forget the looks on their faces; it was a real finger-down-the-throat moment.

I refused to let my kids dictate how to run my life. I invited Tony for family occasions in spite of my kids' objections. But I was very nervous about explaining this new man to my parents, especially my father.

The first night Tony met my parents, Dad started in on him immediately. "Who is this guy?" he asked me when Tony had left the room. "What does he want?" Then, "I don't like him. He's after something!"

My mother was completely charmed by him. Maybe it's because I told her everything about him and our relationship. She totally approved. At least I had one ally.

After an "appropriate" amount of time, Tony and I decided to tell all of the kids—his and mine—that we were going to be married. That went over like a lead balloon.

Tony's kids were also reeling from their parents' divorce and were dealing with issues of their own. Tony had been with his ex-wife, Penny, for more than twenty years. I didn't stop to take into account the rich family history that had been created over those two decades, a history in which I was never involved. Tony's family had been torn apart as completely as mine.

When Tony told his kids that we were going to be married, they didn't take it well, to say the least. They were always very polite and kind to me, but they let us know exactly how they felt, which was *way* less than thrilled.

My kids were basket cases. Kathryn would look at Tony in an odd and disapproving way. She would walk around him and stop to look at his behind, as if she were looking for something.

"What in the world are you looking for?" I finally asked her.

"Well, Dad told me he was the devil, and I was looking for his tail!" she exclaimed, her big brown eyes larger than normal.

"Oka-a-a-y," I said in a calm voice. "So what do you think?"

She contemplated for a moment, and then said, "I don't think he's the devil. Can I go live with Daddy?"

Zach's reaction was equally disturbing. He completely shut down and refused to participate in anything.

To our great relief, whenever we gathered all of the children together, they were wonderful to each other. Anne, Mark, and Denis Thomopoulos went out of their way to be loving and supportive to Zach and Kathryn DeLorean, who, in turn, really liked them. We were lucky, because there are few things worse than sibling rivalry.

Throughout the early years of our marriage, Tony and I fought over two things: Kathryn and Zach. I felt so guilty about the divorce that I didn't want to deal with the soon-to-become-apparent fact that my kids were in desperate need of help. I let them get away with things I shouldn't have. I didn't set rules. I could barely say "no" to them. It was so much easier to say "yes" than to hold my ground and argue. I would give in to them, and then I would have an argument with Tony. I was weak, Tony was not. He could be objective and see things for what they were. He was, and remains, a strict disciplinarian. He sets goals and guidelines and sticks to them. We would butt heads all the time and argue to the point where I wanted to walk out because I couldn't take the pressure. I always felt he was picking on my kids and my lack of parenting skills. It made me feel inadequate.

I became overprotective and undermined Tony's decisions when I should have joined him to present a united front. It caused major problems for us as a couple. Deep down, I knew he was right. I just wanted my kids to love me and not leave me for their father—a move they constantly threatened.

Eventually, my kids ended up splitting time between our home in L.A. and their father's in New York. When they became unbearable, I shipped them off to their dad. They were always happy to go. When John couldn't handle them anymore, he sent them back to me. Tony would set ground rules, and they always agreed to them. They would be happy to be back, until they decided that they no longer wanted to play by our rules. At that point, we would start the cycle all over again, sending the kids between coasts.

When Tony and I recall those stressful times, I profoundly regret that I was not stronger in my commitment to make us work as a family. I know the moving back and forth damaged Kathryn and Zach deeply, and I blame myself.

I had hoped that Tony, Kathryn, and Zach would bond. In reality, they haven't. Is that all right? Yes. I now recognize that our blended clans are never going to be the fairy-tale family unit that I'd imagined. I had hoped my kids would regard Tony as a father figure. I gave up on that dream too. Now I settle merely for them to be kind to one another.

Kathryn and Zach are grown now. As adults, they are very respectful of the home that Tony and I share with them. They wouldn't have it any other way.

——— ✿ ———

If only I could have foreseen all of the wonderful things ahead of us as a family, I wouldn't have been so anxious to have everything be perfect. I wish I had known that one day I would grow to look upon my stepchildren as a part of my true family and that I would love them as my own. I wish I had known how my heart would burst with pride and excitement at their accomplishments, and how my heart would break when they experienced disappointments. I wish I had known that it was fine to argue and disagree without worrying that they wouldn't love me.

I never anticipated the overwhelming feeling of love that I experienced for my stepdaughter Anne in the hospital room after I gave birth to her sister Alex. As I'll discuss in the next chapter, I had a birthing room, and the doctor told me I could bring in two people. I asked Anne if she would share in the experience. I respected her and desperately wanted her to accept me. She agreed to be there with me.

She stepped into the delivery room dressed in her hospital greens, including that silly-looking shower cap they make everyone wear. She took her place beside me and gently held my hand or caressed my forehead as her father frantically barked orders at me. When at last I delivered Alexandra, the doctor lifted her up and laid her on my stomach. It was a freeze-frame moment, a singular perfect second in time. As I reached to touch my baby for the first time, I felt warm drops of water on my forehead. I looked up to see Annie looking down at me, still caressing my hair, shedding huge tears. She was overwhelmed. She bent over to kiss her sister, then kissed me and said, "Thank you, this was amazing. I love my little sister so much. I'll always remember this moment. I can't wait to some day have a baby of my own. Because now I'm not afraid."

That was the turning point in our relationship. Up until then, we had always been cordial towards one another, but we never quite bonded. Alexandra was the little messenger who brought Anne and I together. Two-and-a-half years later, we were back in the delivery room to bring Arianna into the world.

Ten years later, Annie returned the favor when she gave birth to her daughter, Claire. Even though we are not related by blood, these two women own my heart. I feel the same towards my two stepsons, Denis and Mark. We started off wobbly, but ended up close. I get excited when I know they're coming over. They have been loving brothers to their two new sisters and supportive of me.

I'm truly blessed.

—— ✿ ——

As this book goes to press, Tony and I have been married for nineteen years. Throughout much of this time, I had to keep reminding myself that I was a mature adult, and I needed to find a way to unite our clan into a true family. Bringing us all together was very important to me. I loved Tony so much that I wanted to love everything that was important to him.

Yet I've also learned that uniting a family is hard work. It's a long, sometimes painful process that can't be rushed. There will always be bumps in the road, but we've learned to enjoy the journey together. I love my husband, children, stepchildren, and grandchildren more than anything. It is from them that I draw my strength. It's not about my fantasies anymore; it's about them and the reality of everyday life.

Ultimately, life is the best teacher. Here's what I have learned through my stepparenting experience:

- Work with your spouse to set the ground rules together, well before you blend your families.
- Set boundaries, not only for you as parents, but also for your kids.
- Make your children take ownership of their mistakes.
- Be sure that you and your spouse communicate with one another on a daily basis.
- Do not create any room for animosity or resentment. The kids will sense it, and use it to pit you and your spouse against one another.
- Remember that unless you are united as a couple, you are heading for a fall.
- If your children are struggling, get them counseling as soon as possible.
- Don't ever forget that *The Brady Bunch* is just a television show.

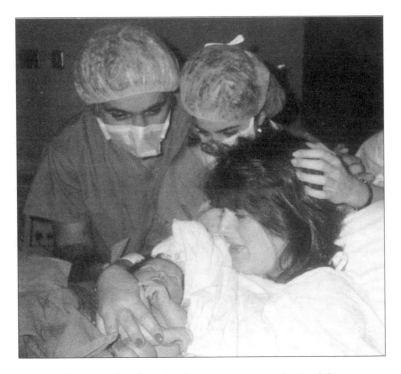

Tony and my stepdaughter Annie were my support in the delivery room as I gave birth to Alexandra. The joy I felt that day was indescribable.

CHAPTER 6

Selective Memory: The Delivery Room Revisited

I AM LOST IN A PICTURE of John, Kathryn, and me in the maternity ward when Alexandra jolts me back to reality with a healthy nudge. She's holding another baby picture, and this one is hers. I remember that one like it was yesterday, just like every mother does.

After Kathryn's birth, I was lucky enough to experience childbirth two more times, with Alexandra and Arianna. It's amazing, no matter what you experience during your turn at giving birth, you forget the pain, anxiety, and trauma and are willing to do it again—sometimes many times.

I got married again at age thirty-five, to the man of my dreams and my true soul mate, Tony. He had three children from his previous marriage, and I had two. He was content with his brood, and I had my hands full with mine. Just the same, the thought of having children together was appealing, and we believed it could only strengthen our already wonderful relationship.

I desperately wanted to have children with Tony, and a year-and-a-half into our marriage, I experienced that familiar dull pulling in my lower abdomen. *(Hmm!)* I bought a home pregnancy kit and sat in my bathroom reading the instructions over and over. I didn't dare make a mistake. My heart was racing, and I eagerly hoped that the test would be positive. Almost immediately after I wet the litmus paper, it came up positive! I couldn't believe it!

But before I shared the news with Tony, I wanted to be absolutely certain. So I went to see my doctor to have him confirm the home test. I was *dying* to tell Tony, but I had to be sure.

I played the fairy tale out in my mind. The doctor would call me back and say, "It's positive! You're pregnant." I'd be elated, naturally! I'd call Tony and tell him to come home from work *immediately* to share some "exciting news." Being the perceptive Wonder Husband that he is, he would immediately know the nature of my news. Of course, he'd leave everything and rush right home. He would burst through the door with a bouquet of my favorite flowers and a small velvet box with a diamond in it. I'd run to his arms and he'd sweep me up and kiss me madly. When we came up for air, I'd say, "Honey, guess what? We're going to have a baby." We'd both be so excited we'd hardly be able to contain ourselves! We'd want to share the news with the world!

If only! In reality, the doctor said, "You tested positive. You're pregnant, congratulations!" *Okay, my fantasy is working out.* Then he continued, "Of course, you realize because of your age (I was thirty-six), it's best that we do an amniocentesis to see if the baby has Down syndrome."

That popped my balloon right there. "Uh-h-h . . . sure," I said, still in shock over being pregnant in the first place. "Isn't amniocentesis the test where they stick a foot-long needle into your abdomen to extract amniotic fluid?" I asked, my voice shaking.

"Piece of cake," the doctor reassured me. *Where have I heard that before?*

I set aside my fears for the moment. First, I had to share this wonderful news with the love of my life! I just couldn't wait to tell Tony, so I called him at work. He didn't have a chance to finish saying hello when I blurted out, "I just came from the doctor's office and we're going to have a baby!"

I waited for a response. I heard nothing. Total silence.

To say the least, he was completely shocked. Though we had talked about having children, he really thought that since I had had such a difficult time conceiving in the past, I probably wouldn't be able to get pregnant. He just wasn't prepared for the news.

Ten years after the birth of my first child, here I was, pregnant again. I was older, wiser, and better prepared for what lay ahead.

In my third month, I had the amniocentesis. When Tony and I arrived at the doctor's office, I was nervous because I knew they were going to stick that humongous needle into me. I soon found out that the actual test isn't half as scary as what they put you through *before* the procedure.

You have to answer reams of questions about your overall health, and they ask you extensive questions about your family history. Questions like, "Do you have anyone in your family who's insane?" *Who doesn't?*

"Anyone who suffers from drug addictions, alcoholism, breast cancer, uterine cancer, brain cancer, lung cancer, any cancer, heart disease, diabetes, multiple sclerosis, cerebral palsy, lupus . . . ?" *Does this list never end? If I say yes to at least two, does this mean we should rethink this whole idea of having a baby?*

The nurse began telling me my options. *My options!* All I wanted to know was the sex of my baby so I could decorate the nursery and buy the right baby clothes. After a two-hour, in-your-face interrogation, she told me the risks of having the amniocentesis. "One of the risks is miscarriage," she said as she smiled and instructed me to put on a hospital gown.

So there I was, lying on a hospital gurney in a darkened room. I was a little queasy and not at all comfortable, knowing the doctor was going to extract fluid from my uterus.

What if he punches a hole in the baby's head? What if he stabs the baby in the eye with that needle? How is he ever going to see where he's going?

I started to panic. I wanted out! I decided to take my chances with a precancerous, alcoholic, drug-addicted baby! Tony reassured me that everything would be fine. He reminded me that this procedure was done all the time. "They have to tell you all that stuff to satisfy their lawyers," he said. "Relax!"

Before we got started, the doctor explained each step of the procedure to me. "Do you have any questions?" he asked when he finished.

"Yes," I said. "Just one. How will you know where to put the needle so you won't poke the baby with it?"

He said that I'd be hooked up to an ultrasound machine, which would allow us to see the baby in the uterus. He explained that he would actually push the baby out of the way as he guided the needle in. And with those words, he took out a gigantic needle and actually said, "Now this won't hurt a bit."

I held on to Tony's hand as we watched the baby on the monitor. We were overwhelmed to see this tiny thing floating there. Right away, Tony asked if the doctor could spot a penis anywhere. *What is it with these guys?* They actually took the time to look really hard. I got impatient. "Could we please proceed?" I asked.

The doctor marked the spot where the needle would enter and asked me not to move or breathe too much. No problem there. I took a deep breath as the needle entered the right side of my abdomen, and I felt a not-so-pleasant pressure followed by a puncture. The pressure was uncomfortable, but I was too scared to say or do anything. I broke out into a cold sweat and just waited for it to be over. Thankfully, it didn't take that long to fill the syringe and extract the needle.

"Go home, go to bed, and stay there for at least twenty-four hours in case of any bleeding," the doctor instructed. Of course, I started worrying about all the horrible things the nurse said *could* happen.

One long week later, I received the news. *A girl!* Tony and I were thrilled. We already knew that we would name her Alexandra.

The advances in medicine are amazing. When I was growing up, we didn't know the sex of a baby until it was born. Here I was only a few weeks pregnant and I already knew that we were going to have a girl and that we'd call her Alexandra.

The rest of the pregnancy was pretty normal. Again, I couldn't get past the idea of carrying for more than six months. Again, the last trimester was a killer. I developed leg cramps beyond reason. They came in the middle of the night, and I had to get Tony to turn me over on my side and hoist me up and help me walk to relieve the cramps. He said it was like walking a baby elephant. That did wonders for my ego.

I developed cravings for corn on the cob and English muffins, and I had to put tons of butter and salt on everything I ate! I ate about eight ears of corn on the cob a day and at least six English muffins. That's on top of everything else I ate. I got up to my magic maternity number again: 185 pounds.

In my ninth month, I was once again told to avoid hot baths and sex. I eliminated the hot baths, but Tony was another story. He just navigated his way around and managed to have a great time in spite of the warnings.

When I had less than three weeks to go, Tony and I went to the movies. During the movie, I kept experiencing tightening in my lower abdomen. I brushed it off as Braxton Hicks contractions, which is when the muscles of the uterus tighten for short periods of time to get ready for the "big day." I just thought I was having more tightening than usual.

After the movie, I went to bed, but I couldn't fall asleep because the pains were coming every ten minutes. It finally dawned on me around three in the morning that I was actually having contractions. I woke Tony. He automatically got up to hoist me up to take me for my walk. I quickly explained that I was in labor and we needed to go to the hospital.

We got dressed and called the neighbors to watch Zach and Kathryn. I tried in vain to reach my parents, but their line was busy. I kept trying right up to the moment we left for the hospital. I continued to call from the car, but their line remained busy. I insisted that we go by their house because it was weird that their line was busy all this time.

"Are you nuts?" Tony said. "You're in labor!"

"I don't care," I said, taking a deep, cleansing breath because the contractions were starting to hurt. "I want my mother. Besides, something is wrong. Their phone shouldn't be busy at three in the morning."

By now the contractions were coming every seven minutes. But I was determined to see what was up with my parents. We pulled up to their house and I tried to get out of the car, but I was like a helium balloon stuck in a crawl space. Tony tried to help get me out. No such luck.

"Please go to the house to see if my parents have been murdered, and be careful not to wake the neighbors!" I said. He shook his head in amazement. "Where do you come up with these sick scenarios?" he asked.

"Be careful and don't bang too loudly on the door so you don't scare Mom, just in case they're not dead," I said from my command post in the car. After all, it *was* three in the morning.

"No, Tony, wait!" I whisper-yelled. "I'm having a contraction!"

Tony looked at me, exasperated. "What the hell do you want me to do?"

After the contraction stopped, I managed to crawl out of the car and ring the doorbell. My dad answered the door with a baseball bat. Yikes!

"What are you guys doing here?" he demanded. "What the hell's wrong with you?"

Tony told him to put down the bat. "We're going to the hospital to have the baby," he said.

"Why didn't you call first?" Dad asked, puzzled.

By now, Mom was downstairs, also wanting to know why we were there. She, too, wanted to know why we hadn't called first.

"We tried, but the line was always busy, and I got scared," I explained.

It turned out that the phone was just knocked off the hook. One problem solved, another one on the horizon. Because by then, I was on the front lawn in a fetal position, moaning and realizing that I was in very big trouble. The contractions were coming on stronger. Everybody got me to my feet and into the car. My parents said they'd meet us at the hospital.

This time, I was preregistered. We made sure of that. I got a room right away, and I was already four centimeters dilated. The doctor said, "You're not leaving until we have a baby!"

The doctor also asked if I wanted an epidural. "Absolutely!" I said.

Enter the anesthesiologist, whom I called Dr. Mushroom Head. He was wearing green scrubs, gauze slippers, and a cap that made him look like a mushroom. He was very sweet and attentive. He explained how he was going to insert this six-inch needle into my spine to numb the pain of the contractions.

What's going to numb the pain of the needle going into my spine? He explained everything to me before he proceeded, but I felt very nervous in spite of his pep talk. He gave me Novocain to numb the area, which stung, and then inserted the needle. He was done before I even knew he had started. I felt only pressure, and that was survivable.

I went through twelve pain-free hours. I continued to dilate. Tony, my parents, my friends, and my kids came in and out of my room all day. The anesthesiologist stood by my side pretty much the whole day, becoming my new best friend. He entertained Tony and me and made sure we had anything we needed.

Wow! What service!

Around six that evening, things started to get intense. The birthing time was drawing close, and my new friend reduced the anesthetic so I could start to "feel a bit and be able to push."

My legs were completely paralyzed because of the epidural. At one point, my leg fell off the table and I wasn't able to bring it back up on my own. Tony had to help lift it back. I didn't appreciate his remark that he needed a crane to lift it!

Doctor Mushroom Head came in for a final check. As I was lying there with my legs in the stirrups, he casually placed one elbow on the top of my knee and leaned on it. Then he diverted his attention away from me over to Tony. "You know, I've written a script." he said.

Oh, for heaven's sake! This guy has been kissing my butt all this time so he can submit a script to Tony! At the time, Tony was the president of United Artists Studios.

By then I was feeling uncomfortable as I realized the contractions were painful again. The anesthesiologist's attention was stuck on Tony, not me.

"I'll send it to you tomorrow," Dr. Mushroom Head offered. "Will you read it?"

Tony just stared at him, so annoyed at the impropriety of this that he replied in a stern and definitely annoyed tone, "No."

By this time, I started to feel the contractions. "Don't you worry, I'll read it as soon as we pop this baby out," I told him. "I'm sure it's great. I'll make sure he gives it his full attention. Speaking of attention, do you think you can give me a little more 'juice,' because I can really start to feel pain?"

It was at this point that my ob-gyn, who was clearly annoyed at the anesthesiologist's behavior, said, "We better go into the operating room in case we need to take the baby by C-section. Just a precaution."

"You can take two people with you," he said.

I decided on Tony and my stepdaughter Anne.

Both donned their hospital greens and took their places beside me. As the contractions became ever more intense, Tony would run to the end of the bed to see if the baby was coming, then run back to my shoulder to lift me so I could push, and then turn around and run back again to see if the baby was crowning. "Not yet," he'd say in his best cheerleader voice. "Damn. Okay, let's try this!" Then he'd stand at my side, lifting my shoulders and cupping his arms under my knees and actually folding me into a "V" position. I looked at my doctor, begging him to stop this maniac. Meanwhile, Anne was gently caressing my forehead. She became my calming force.

The baby's head finally crowned, and the doctor actually said to Tony, "Lay across her stomach and help push the baby out!"

Tony did this three times. Because of the epidural, I wasn't experiencing much pain except for the weight of Tony's body on my belly. I thought for sure the baby would be flattened. The third time it worked, as we both pushed our daughter into the world.

Alexandra Thomopoulos was born November 25, 1986. She weighed eight pounds, eleven ounces. No C-section needed; she just slid right out.

I never had the opportunity to breastfeed my first baby, Kathryn, because I was in so much pain from the C-section. My doctor gave me a shot so my milk wouldn't come in. I was disappointed but determined that if I ever gave birth to a second child, I would definitely breastfeed.

After Alexandra was born, the doctor said it would take about three days for my milk to come in. Until then, my body would be producing nutrient-rich colostrum, nature's perfect food for newborns. The moment they placed Alex on my stomach, I couldn't *wait* to start feeding her. But she was so exhausted from her birth that she immediately fell asleep, and I had to wait patiently for her to wake up. When she finally awoke, I brought her to my breast to start nursing her. We navigated quite a bit while she tried to make contact with a nipple that was bigger than her face. When she finally latched on, my toes curled in pain.

Oh my God, this hurts! I figured I'd get over it. The nurse said that once the baby started to suckle, it would stimulate "let down"—whatever that meant—and nursing would feel better. Well, it didn't! When my milk came in three days later, I was horrified! My breasts were bigger than the baby. I had to hold them to keep her from suffocating while she nursed. She was fussy and wouldn't take the milk. Because she wasn't eating, I became anxious and worried that she would die of malnutrition. The more anxious I became, the more she refused to eat.

When she didn't eat, the nurse would come in with a pump to extract the milk. She used a contraption that looked like a baby Hoover vacuum cleaner. She placed it over my nipple, turned it on, and before I knew it, my entire nipple was sucked into a long cylinder as the machine started to pump. Now I know how cows feel when they're being milked!

I couldn't take it anymore. I decided to bottle-feed. I asked the nurse if she could give me a shot to dry up the milk, like they did after my first pregnancy. "That's not possible," she said. "Once your milk comes in, you just have to wait it out. All you can do is bind your breasts down really tight, and in a few days the pain will begin to simmer down."

Simmer down? What is that supposed to mean? I wondered. I had never seen breasts so large on any human. I'm normally a 36C, but they must have *quadrupled* in size. To make matters worse, they became engorged. The milk got stuck in the milk ducts, which blocked everything and made my already tender breasts hurt even more.

It wasn't long before I understood what the nurse meant by "simmer down." My breasts were actually *hot*. No, I don't mean hot looking; I mean hot to the touch. I bought some rubber surgery gloves, filled them with ice, and tucked two in either side of the cups of my bra.

What horrified me most was that my breasts had become two perfectly round, huge hemispheres. My skin was stretched so far that it was shiny. Tony thought they were amazing and actually had the gall to ask me if my breasts were going to stay like that.

Not only was I uncomfortable with my breasts, but my episiotomy was killing me, and I had horrible cramps from my uterus trying to shrink. I was sleep-deprived, experiencing post-partum depression, and convinced I would never feel normal again.

I became paranoid and started checking on Alexandra every fifteen minutes to make sure that she was still breathing. I insisted that she sleep right next to my bed because I was afraid I wouldn't hear her. Boy was I wrong about that. I heard her loud and clear every time she cried.

—— 🐎 ——

No matter what kind of experience you have delivering your baby, somehow you find yourself wanting to have another one. As the months go by, your memory plays tricks on you. You forget everything about the pain, and convince yourself that because you did it before, you know exactly what to expect. You're sure that it will be different "this time."

My last baby came at the busiest time of my life, when I was doing three television shows all at once. A typical day meant that I would be on the air live from 7:00 A.M. to 9:00 A.M. for ABC's *Home Show*. From 9:00 A.M. to 10:00 A.M., I would shoot *A.M. Los Angeles*. After that, I would be in production meetings until 1 P.M., when I would head to a different studio to shoot another ABC program, *Incredible Sunday*.

I didn't have time to worry about my pregnancy or morning sickness. Between taking care of Alexandra and working, I had no time to think of all the normal things you think about when you're pregnant. Luckily, this was my third pregnancy and I knew what to expect.

Everything went smoothly and right on target. I had my amniocentesis and went through the same ordeal that I'd gone through the last time. I tried to convince the nurses at the clinic that I didn't need the interrogation again because I had just gone through one eighteen months earlier. It seemed more efficient to skip right to the part with the long needle, but the nurses insisted on inflicting their whole inquisition on me again. A week later, I found out I was having another little girl. We were thrilled.

Three weeks before I was to give birth, I left for work as usual. Well, not exactly as usual. Tony and I always discussed our plans for the day, telling each other what we were going to be doing and where we would be at different times. It was especially important towards the end of the pregnancy to keep in contact in case I needed to go to the hospital. For some reason, I forgot to ask him about his itinerary that morning.

After the *Home Show* taping was finished, I went to lunch with Woody Fraser, the show's producer and also a friend. We ate at a funky Tex-Mex restaurant. The food was phenomenal. We both love to eat, and we ordered everything on the menu. I was in heaven. After sampling each and every one of the desserts, I finished my feast with a cappuccino. As I took my last sip and placed the cup on the saucer, I heard a loud "pop!" Suddenly I felt my uterus contracting, and I realized my pants and chair were soaking wet.

I quietly and gently leaned over to Woody and said, "Now Woody, I don't want you to get nervous or say anything, okay?" (Woody is known for his theatrics.) "My water just broke, and I forgot to ask Tony where he would be at lunchtime. I need you to take me to the hospital if I can't locate him," I continued.

With that, he stood up and *yelled* so the entire restaurant could hear him, "Her water broke! Her water broke!" So much for privacy.

The whole restaurant erupted in applause and I became very self-conscious as I waddled out the door with my pants soaking wet and leaking amniotic fluid on the floor. I tried to call Tony. He was at lunch, as was his secretary. I had no idea where he was or how to find him (we didn't carry cell phones then), and I realized that Woody was going to have to take me to the hospital.

This is not the way it happens in the fairy tale. Your husband is supposed to take you to the hospital. You have to be nervous and anxious together and savor every moment, so when it's over you can relive the memories together, right? Instead, I found myself with a very nice man whom I didn't really know all that well. He was holding my hand and reassuring me by telling me, "Don't worry. I'll be there for you."

On the drive to the hospital, my contractions started coming every three minutes, and I mean *hard*. With each contraction, I leaked more fluid on the front seat of Woody's fabulous new car. Amniotic fluid was everywhere. The only absorbent thing he had in his car was a box of tissues, which I used up in about two minutes. To make matters worse, we were in downtown L.A., and the hospital was at least forty-five minutes away.

We arrived just in time for them to whisk me into the delivery room. Tony was still nowhere to be found. The staff prepped me and reassured me that the baby would come soon. Woody came in, dressed in a hospital gown. He took my hand and said, "Focus on the ceiling and take a deep, cleansing breath." I started to laugh at how strange everything had become: to be delivering a baby and have a man who is not my husband holding me and telling me to focus and take that all-important deep, cleansing breath. I stared at the ceiling, where someone had drawn a heart and written inside it the words, "Don't worry. Be happy!" Just then, Tony burst into the delivery room. Like Superman, he announced in a deep baritone voice, "Don't worry Woody, I'll take it from here!" *Oh, great. He tells* Woody *not to worry!*

Then, the door burst open again. This time it was a man dressed in green scrubs from head to toe, his cap askew. He was holding a bottle and a huge needle. My worst fears were coming true. It was Dr. Mushroom Head, the script-writing anesthesiologist I'd encountered that last time I was about to deliver. Throughout my pregnancy, I wasn't worried about giving birth. I was worried about another encounter with this anesthesiologist—and here he was, right in front of me.

I looked over at Tony. "Don't worry, I'll be there with you," he said. *That was supposed to make me feel better?*

"He's not sticking that needle up *your* spine!" I said, cursing Tony for not reading the anesthesiologist's script and making it into a movie.

The anesthesiologist/screenwriter asked me to roll over on my side and curl up into a fetal position. I did this gladly because the labor pains were starting to really hurt. But those pains were nothing compared to when he stuck that big needle in me. I actually saw stars! My OB-GYN had him replaced immediately.

As I lay there staring at the ceiling, I thought back to when I was little. *Why was it that my deliveries never came out the way I used to imagine they would?* I thought childbirth was going to be like in the movies. My husband would be a darling idiot and forget the bags and run all over the place looking for the car keys, even though he was holding them in his hand. At the hospital, he would pace back and forth in the waiting room with the rest of the family, everyone looking nervous and scared. I used to wonder what they were so nervous about; they weren't the ones lying on a table trying to pass something as big as a bowling ball from their body.

In my childhood imaginings, the mother-to-be would be whisked away to a secret room where you could hear moans and screams for no more than five minutes. These moans would be followed by a cinematic slap and the garbled cry of an infant. When these scenes were played on television, I would always look over at my parents because that last part always made my mother cry. My parents would hold hands and reminisce about when they had us. How dopey I thought they were.

Dopey until I had the real experience. The real labor pains. The real concerns about whether or not my baby would be healthy. The reality of facing biology: The baby must come out, and there are only two ways out of there! *Will I be able to do it naturally, or will I need a C-section? Will it hurt, and will I scream like those women on TV and in the movies?*

Will I love this baby? Will my husband still love me? Will I ever lose this weight? Will I ever feel normal again?

"Concentrate, Cristina, and start pushing," my doctor ordered, snapping me back into the moment. It was my third time at this experience, and we were all anxious to meet the newest member of our growing family. As I started pushing, Tony grabbed his camera and started clicking away.

I could hear him yelling, like some crazed movie director, "Beautiful like that! Yeah, beautiful like that! Oh god, that's so *beautiful!*" He took so many pictures I felt like I was back at a modeling shoot.

What in the world is he going on about? "Will you knock that off?" I yelled. He was so enthralled at photographing the birth that he completely forgot about me.

As the baby's head started to crown, Tony realized he needed to change the film. At this point, he actually said to me, "Hold on, Honey. Don't move!"

Yeah, right, Tony. I'll just hold the head right where it is until you finish changing the film and are ready to resume your photographic documentation of this event.

All of a sudden, I heard Tony scream, "Oh *+^#! Oh no! I don't believe this! No, no, this can't be!"

Why is he so upset? Does he see that something's wrong on the fetal monitor? What does he see? "What is it?" I demanded.

He turned to me with the camera open to reveal there was no film inside. By then, the baby was ready to come out with one more healthy push. "It's too late to do anything about it now," I screamed. "We'll just have to make sure that next time, you have the camera all set up properly."

Tony actually stopped dead in his tracks. He asked the doctor right then and there for the name of a physician who does vasectomies.

Arianna Thomopoulos weighed in at seven pounds, six ounces.

I didn't even attempt to breastfeed.

*Has anyone seen my skis? Vacation mishaps like this
sometimes had me searching for my sanity as well!*

CHAPTER 7

Family Vacations

WHY DOES THE WOMAN in the ad for a tropical vacation look so happy and rested? She is always tanned and usually artfully positioned on a towel in the sand at the edge of the breaking water. The water looks warm, clean, and deeply blue from the reflection of the cloudless sky. It's a perfect contrast to the pure white sand. In her perfectly manicured hand, the woman holds a crystal glass that contains a frosty libation that is the same color as the sea. Lying next to her is a gorgeous guy with broad shoulders and a beautifully cut stomach. He's rubbing suntan oil all over her.

It's at this point that I let my imagination run away. You know that after he oils her sleek body, he will gently take that frosty cold drink from her. He'll set it down with his left hand as his right hand gently lifts her chin to bring her closer to him. Their anxious lips meet, kissing deeply as they are surrounded by the warm, caressing waves of the ocean. The waves lick their bodies, and the tingling sensation of the cool, salty water heightens their passion. They make love right there on the beach.

Afterwards, they head to their hotel suite, where there is a chilled bottle of champagne waiting beside a warm, bubbling Jacuzzi bath. As she places her foot in the steamy water, she can immediately feel the warmth radiate all the way up her long, lean leg.

It is at this point that I put down my magazine and say, "What a crock!" I don't know about you, but when I get home from a vacation, I *need* a vacation. The whole concept of family vacations must have been made up by someone who never had kids. And believe me, I've tried them all—tropical vacations, ski vacations, even the ever-popular theme park vacations.

Tony and I took our first family vacation as a couple when Alex was two-and-a-half years and Arianna was three months old. Along with us were all three of my stepchildren: Anne, Mark, and Denis. We also included Anne's boyfriend—whom I never did see again after that trip, ever—and my two kids from my previous marriage, Kathryn and Zach. Eight kids altogether, ranging in ages from three months to twenty-three years.

We chose Hawaii as our destination. I thought it was my chance to have a *Brady Bunch* vacation. At least that's what I thought in the beginning.

Getting everyone in one space at the same time is always a challenge. So Mom becomes the designated coordinator of *everything*. As such, I make a list of chores that must be done before we leave:

> Empty out the refrigerator.
> Make sure all the windows are closed and locked.
> Call the neighbors to ask the rest of the neighbors to be on
>   extra alert for the neighborhood watch.
> Before taking the pets to the kennel, make sure their shots are
>   up to date. If they're not, the kennel will reject them. Of

course, the shots aren't up to date, so it's off to the vet I go with three dogs who immediately start to shake and pee all over the car the minute we pull into the parking lot and they recognize where they are.

Next, ensure the mail is going to be picked up.

Call the newspaper and tell them not to deliver. That never works. Every time I come home from a vacation, I have fourteen newspapers piled up in the driveway. So much for not letting burglars know no one is at home.

Pack appropriate clothes, including a fresh change of underwear for each day and clean pajamas. Let's not forget acne medication, special shampoo, IDs for everyone, creams, tampons, suntan oil, hairbrushes, toothbrushes in different colors, extra toothbrushes, Beano for the lactose intolerants of our troop (and there are many), deodorant, and sexy lingerie (because inevitably Good Ol' Dad is going to try to nail you somehow). By the way, no one wants to share a suitcase, even though it would reduce the amount of luggage by half.

We all convene on the driveway for the monumental task of trying to fit fourteen pieces of luggage and umpteen carry-ons into three regular-size cars. Two cars had to be borrowed. Next, there is the fight over who is going to ride with whom, all the while trying to remember to separate the kids who will tear each others' hair out.

At the airport, keeping track of the luggage and the kids is a lesson in patience. After you find a skycap—and good luck with that—you must decide what's going onboard and what's being checked. You have to make sure that every piece of checked luggage has a name tag and is given over to the baggage checkers. You must hope and pray nothing gets lost, including the claim check, carry-on luggage, and the kids. One piece, *any* piece, of lost luggage will ruin the *whole* vacation.

After they're unloaded, the cars need to be valet-parked. The older boys volunteer for that job. "Don't forget to bring me the claim checks for the cars!" I scream as they squeal away, drag racing each other to the parking lot.

Once we all convene in the terminal, it will be at least another 40 to 50 minutes before we get through security. Once through the security checkpoint, I dread what I now have to face. Flying economy class should be outlawed. No human being should be subjected to such unconscionable conditions. The airline's strategy of playing supposedly soothing Hawaiian music doesn't help make things any more pleasant, especially when you have kids under four who must be secured in a car seat. In our case, we have two! Just lugging each bulky car seat onto the plane is a chore in itself. You can't turn sideways because you'll bang into whomever is already sitting in the aisle seats. So you have to hoist the seat over your head, along with the diaper bag and other carry-ons that have been weighing down your shoulders.

As you inch down the aisle, you get stuck every few feet because all your gear makes it impossible to fit between the seats. By the way: *Who has the baby?* Once you find her, good luck in trying to get her into the car seat. How can babies make their bodies so rigid and straight that they actually slide right through your arms, off of the car seat, and onto the floor? You try to pick them up, but their little bodies are so stiff you can't seem to get a grip. They just won't bend, and you can't make them.

Once you finally manage to get a handle on them, you try ever so hard to inch their little tushies into the seat. They just won't have it, so they start to scream bloody murder. Not the little "I don't wanna!" scream, but the extra high, extra shrill, extra *loud* scream! (*Okay, just kill me now!*) Everyone around you gives you "The Look." Oh, you know which one. The one that says, *Is this kid going to cry the whole time?* I am totally alone. My whole family looks at me as if they don't know me. I ask the flight attendant if she could please warm up the milk for a bottle, but she just looks at me with disdain. Besides, she's too busy helping other passengers squeeze themselves into cramped quarters by offering them some more stuff (blankets, pillows, and headsets they charge you for) to take up even more space.

I decide to take matters into my own hands. I remove the baby from the car seat and place her into a soft, pink zippered carrying case. It's a little oval container with cloth handles on the sides and a tiny soft mattress. She seems to like it and settles down immediately. I'm hesitant to give her a bottle because I want to save it for after we take off so she will sleep at least a couple of hours. But because of "The Look" I'm still getting from my fellow inmates, I decide to give her the bottle now.

She falls asleep immediately. I am relieved, perfectly content to just hold her in my arms and be still. Forty minutes pass, and I'm concerned that this quiet time has been spent on the ground and not actually getting somewhere! Finally, we slowly back out of the gate.

We are number sixteen for takeoff!

One hour later, the captain's voice advises us that "We're now number two for takeoff."

That's when the flight attendant comes up to me.

"You'll have to remove the baby and place the bed under the seat," she says.

"Excuse me," I say. "This is not a bed, it's a blanket with a zipper."

"FAA regulations," she says. "Now please place the container under the seat in front of you. Or we're not going anywhere."

"You don't understand," I say, trying to explain as gently and quietly as I can. "If I remove the baby from her *blanket*, she'll wake up and then we'll all be sorry."

She shoots me a glare that makes me want to smack her. Then, loudly, so everyone can hear, she screams, "It is against federal regulations to have a carry-on on your lap during takeoff and landing. If you do not remove the child from the carry-on, we will have to go back to the gate and remove you from the plane."

Once again, I try to explain that this is a soft blanket and not a carry-on. But it's all to no avail. Now I get the *other* look from my traveling buddies. The one that says, *Lady, if you make us go back to the gate, we will kill you!* I give in and remove my daughter from the blanket. Not liking this one bit, she starts to cry. As we finally take off, the roaring sound of the engines mercifully drowns out her wailing.

Once we are airborne, the person in front of me reclines his seat—all the way back. Not only do I have a crying baby in my lap, but I now have a 235-pound man with his gigantic, sweaty head sitting directly under my chin!

I can't move. My husband takes pity on me and takes the baby and recruits the other kids to help out. Everything is going just fine until I hear those dreaded words: "Mommy, I have to go potty!" I have an aversion to public restrooms and now I am deeply distressed. Normally, I can get through it with a minimal amount of anxiety, but when you're 35,000 feet in the air and you're sharing the toilet with 150 people, it's not pretty. With my boy, it was always easy. You just hoist him up and let him take aim. With girls, it's a whole other story. I don't even want to go into it. Besides, I need to get this task done before they start the meal service.

Of course, trying to eat your so-called "meal" is impossible. Once you put your tray table down, you're stuck in that one position. You stay that way until you are "released" by the flight attendant, who will eventually remove your tray—just not before all 150 passengers have been served. Forget the fact that you received your meal first and you've been finished for about forty minutes.

It's tough to keep the kids in their seats. If one escapes, you're in trouble. They can easily slide right under the tray table onto the floor and out the aisle. You, on the other hand, are *so* stuck and can't escape without major complications.

The only bright side is that the kids likely won't get far because the cart and flight attendants are planted firmly in the aisle. If you have to use the toilet, good luck: There is no way to get to the lavatory without moving the cart either up or down the long aisle. You don't dare ask them to do so for fear of lynching from hungry passengers who hate you anyway. At least that's what it feels like.

It's a long flight, no matter how you cut it. Unless the kids sleep, which they rarely do, you are the sole entertainment. With all of my in-flight training, I'm certain that if I auditioned for *Sesame Street*, I'd get the gig!

After what seems like days, instead of hours, we finally reach our destination: beautiful, tropical Honolulu, Hawaii. We try to get out of the plane as fast as we can because we need to catch the puddle-jumper to the next island. Our window of opportunity is twenty-five minutes. We wait patiently as the other passengers start to deplane, inching their way down the aisle ever so slowly. I'm sure we're going to miss our flight and be stuck at the airport with nowhere to go and no luggage. By now, all I want to do is sit in a normal chair and be able to pee sitting down.

When we get off the plane, we run—huffing and puffing—to the gate for the plane that will take us to our final destination. I nearly faint when I see the plane. It has propellers! *Only two!* The body of the plane is so small I immediately feel a sense of doom. Not because I'm afraid it's going to crash, but because I know there will be many of my new enemies from our last flight. After we climb the stairs with all our gear, I turn the corner to find our seats. We have to bend over so we don't hit our heads on the ceiling. (*If only I could just disappear.*) We start the whole ritual again, getting ready for takeoff with everyone glaring at me, letting me surmise that I'd best keep things under control. Once we are airborne, the flight takes only twenty minutes. *Thank you, God!* When we arrive in Maui, we descend the staircase of the plane and are greeted by beautiful, smiling Hawaiian women who adorn us with leis. The air smells so sweet and it is so comfortably warm that I get a sense of almost immediate relief. It has taken a total of eleven-and-a-half hours to get to this point—we could have flown to Japan!—but I'm feeling optimistic that the rest of our journey will go smoothly.

We retrieve our luggage, and miraculously, it's all there. Then we pile into the waiting vans and head for the hotel. We check in. Our rooms are not ready. Why would they be?!

"After three, after three," we're told.

Let's see, it's 12:30. The kids aren't hungry because they ate the crap on the plane. They're hyper. I suggest they all go down to the beach and relax while we figure out what to do with the luggage. They return fifteen minutes later.

"We can't find anywhere to sit on the beach!" they scream in unison. "Everything's taken!"

I finally lose it. "This is Hawaii," I bellow. "It's big. That's the Pacific Ocean. It's wide. Go out there and find someplace to park your butts!"

They manage to find a very nice spot not so close to the hotel, and we all wait for our rooms until *precisely* 3 o'clock.

The kids get to their respective rooms and immediately unleash the contents of their suitcases. I try to explain what a dresser drawer is to the younger ones, but they don't get the concept. The floor is their "dresser drawer," and they pile and strew their belongings around their room. Somehow, magically, they always manage to find whatever it is they need. But I can't live like this! We order room service because my husband "forgot" to make a reservation at the restaurant, so we can't get a table until 10:45. The kitchen closes at 11:00.

Before we go to bed, I call downstairs to reserve two cabanas and umbrellas for our day at the beach in the morning. The concierge informs me that they do not take reservations. It's on a first-come, first-served basis. I start to worry about how I'm going to get everyone settled in one happy spot. I decide I'm going to get up really early so I can set up the cabanas and umbrellas for my little tribe. I want everything to be perfect.

It's 5:00 A.M. An alarm goes off in my brain. I'm still on L.A. time. I leap out of bed, thinking I'm going to have "alone time" to fix up my beach huts. When I get downstairs, I head toward the cabanas. I grab a ton of towels and head off to stake my claim. But I'm apparently too late. Covering every lounge chair are bathrobes, magazines, and those annoying plastic slippers that the hotel gives you. There's not a single lounger left to be had. (Now I know how the kids felt when we arrived.) I look around for help, but there is absolutely no one on the beach. It seems that everyone else had the same idea and came down early, staked their claim, and simply went back to bed.

How early do you have to wake up here? I realize that most of the guests are from the mainland; depending on where they live, their body clocks are hours ahead. Let's see, I figure, *If you're from New York, you probably got up around midnight!* I look for the cabana boys. None to be found. I soon discover that they don't come on duty until 8:00 A.M. I decide to set myself up under a palm tree.

Off I go to find the perfect tree, one that will provide enough shade during the day. I dump all of the towels and the huge beach bag. It's filled with magazines, suntan lotion, sand toys, and miscellaneous items we might need during the course of the day. I line up all ten towels in a row and take great pride in how uniform it all looks. (*There's something wrong with me, I know.*) I head back up to the pool area to find umbrellas. Two by two, I drag these top-heavy contraptions to the sand and place them strategically around my camp. Everything looks great. Pleased with myself, I go back to our room.

My tribe is starting to stir. I suggest we head down to the hotel restaurant for the breakfast buffet. We're rested and anxious to start our fun-filled family vacation. So we all navigate a maze of seemingly endless corridors until we finally reach the elevators. The hotel, I will soon learn, has 650 rooms serviced by only two banks of elevators, so we end up waiting a very long time. The smaller kids are so bored they start to poke holes in the ashtrays that have the hotel logo strategically and neatly placed in the sand. They leave their initials.

The elevator finally arrives, announcing itself with the obligatory ring. We discover we can't all fit in together because it will hold only eight people. Already inside is a really big, really hairy man with his Hawaiian shirt wide open. He takes up two spaces. He's wearing one of those tiny red European bikini bottoms—tinier than a Speedo—and flip-flops. His belly is hanging over his tiny swimsuit. He has on heavy suntan oil and strong aftershave. The aroma is so sickeningly sweet that it makes our heads spin. If there were bees in the elevator, they would be making honey. To make matters worse, as we all squeeze in, Alex has been pushed right in front of the big man, and she's facing him. Her head comes right up to his crotch. She very innocently points to the protrusion in his swimsuit and asks, very loudly, "What's that?"

After what seems like an eternity, the elevator doors open and we spill out as we try to find our way to the dining room. Hostesses the world over must loathe it when you march into the dining room with a party of ten. You can tell by the way they roll their eyes. No matter what time you get there, there is always a line you must stand in before you can even let the hostess know how many people are in your party. She then tells you in a *what-do-you-expect-with-a-party-of-ten* tone, "It'll be at least thirty minutes."

Who wants to wait thirty minutes for breakfast with small children? But, of course, you have no choice. Everyone in every resort hotel seems to want to eat at the same time, especially when it comes to breakfast. Because our party is so large, it takes extra time to set up the table. And even after it's all set and ready, they still keep you waiting.

We start out our day at the buffet, eating every item imaginable. Where else but on a vacation would you eat all of the following for breakfast: sushi, creamed chicken, bacon, sausage, oatmeal, miso soup, eggs benedict, a dollop of macaroni salad, a Belgian waffle, an egg white omelet (made without butter, please), a taste of French toast, Brie, pineapple, mango, papaya, cappuccino, and fresh guava and orange juice? But on a vacation, I do. What is that about?

After breakfast I could just kill myself; I feel so incredibly lousy. I'll start my diet tomorrow.

During the day, it's nearly impossible for me to relax because the little ones cannot be left alone for a millisecond. The hotel has wonderful day care facilities, but I didn't fly all this way to put my kids in day care. Oh no, not me! I'm going to spend real one-on-one time with them. But by 10:30 A.M., I am so exhausted and full from breakfast I can barely move.

I can't sit back by the pool and read. I have to watch the kids because, if I don't, I'm sure they'll drown. And if they go near the ocean, I can't sit on my beach blanket. Unless I'm standing right there with them, I'm absolutely sure they'll be swept out to sea, never to be heard from again.

I get Tony to mind Arianna, who sleeps most of the time anyway. She is happy and content under the shade of a palm tree. Now I find myself digging holes in the sand and burying Alex and Kathryn up to their necks. I'm thinking to myself, *I wonder how long I can leave them in there . . . ?* They think it's the greatest thing in the world. As they jump in and out of the hole a hundred times, Alex inevitably gets sand in her mouth and eyes and starts to cry. She tries to remove the sand with her sandy hands. Now, she's spitting and blind. We head for the ocean to dunk and rinse, but it's all to no avail because now she has salt water in her eyes and it stings.

We decide to head for the outdoor shower. We rinse off, but she's still not happy because she has sand in her bottom. So it's off to the hotel room, which is in the next county, to shower and change bathing suits. It's 11:45 by the time we get back.

By now, Ari is awake and I must include her in all of the reindeer games. The older kids come around and offer some relief, for which I'm grateful. I'm realistic, and I realize that they really want to be left alone to do their own thing. I want to respect that, but only after I know what they're doing and who their new friends are.

"You're overprotective," says Tony. "Can't you just leave them be?" I shoot him a scowl. "Half of the kids aren't even yours," he adds. "So lay off."

So now we have our first vacation fight. It's 12:30 P.M. First day. Nine more days to go.

We split up for lunch. Tony wants to sit under the palm tree and have his meal alone and read in solitude. *Yeah—me too, buddy.* I sit at the kiddie pool with the smaller kids and five hundred other parents with young ones. There are spilled sodas, squashed peanut butter sandwiches, and soggy potato chips everywhere. Everything tastes like Coppertone. The kids love it and are so happy to be living like this. I start to take photos to immortalize our time together. It is really sweet to see the kids so happy and having such a wonderful time. It makes me feel good inside that we can actually have this time together. I realize that this time is really for them, and us, as a family.

I have a decision to make: I can sit and moan about how everything may not be exactly how I imagined it from the brochure as I keep scanning the beach for that perfect spot, or I can just go with the flow and enjoy this special time with my family.

I choose to go with the flow. Ten fun-filled days!

By the time we're ready to leave, we've fallen into a routine and into the slower pace that Hawaii affords you. We've learned how to navigate back and forth to our rooms without a map and found the perfect window of opportunity to eat breakfast—after the early birds and before the lunch crowd. I've managed to get to the spa because I caved in and put the girls in the daycare camp for a few hours a day, which they preferred anyway.

Alex liked camp much better than having Mom as her camp

counselor. "At least I didn't have someone constantly rubbing sunblock on me and making me wait after eating before going into the water, and forcing me to wear a stupid hat!" she told me.

We start packing the day before we leave to ensure that we have everything we came with, including all of our newly acquired Hawaiian T-shirts and extra bathing suits. I make sure to look under all the beds, behind drawers, and in between mattresses for lost belongings. As I watch the kids pack, I see all the wrinkled clothes, damp bathing suits, and sandy shoes being shoved into suitcases that now are nearly impossible to close because of all the new goodies. In my mind, I can visualize what my laundry room is going to look like when we get back home.

But first we have to get home (one step at a time). I start to remember that experience, when a voice snaps me back to the present, where I'm surrounded by moving boxes and bags of snapshots and vacation brochures.

"Mom, Mom, don't *go* there!" It's Alex. She's shaking my arm and pulling the Hawaiian vacation brochure from my hand. "Gee, Mom, you get that same look on your face when you do laundry," she says. "Are you okay?"

"Yes, I'm okay," I assure her, as we find yet another shoebox full of vacation memories. I pull out a photograph, and there we are, all lined up in our brand-new ski outfits, looking like we actually know how to ski. The bottom of the box is filled with magazines advertising ski vacations from all over the world, from the Alps to Sun Valley, Idaho. We picked Idaho.

—— ⚸ ——

Once again, I'd succumbed to the ad in the magazine. I can still remember it clearly: A beautiful woman with flowing, shoulder-length dark hair is wearing a headband that says "SKI IDAHO." The headband is the same color as the stripe on her skintight ski outfit. She's flying down a majestic mountain in pure white virgin powder. She is tilting to the left, and over her shoulders you can see just how crisp and perfectly clear blue the sky is.

Right next to her is a hunk of burning love (probably the same guy from the Hawaii ad), a gorgeous guy with broad shoulders and the perfect physique. He's not wearing a ski jacket. Why should he? It's perfect spring skiing weather. He's wearing a one-piece suit that looks like it was painted on. His teeth are so white I don't know where he stops and the snow begins. His well-muscled thighs are bulging from all that skiing, and his arms ripple with athletic muscles. He, too, is tilting to the left, projecting a sense of continuity and fluidity to their movements. You can just picture yourself in the same situation as you plan *your* perfect glide down the mountain!

Your ride down the mountain will end up costing you a pretty penny, especially if you live in a warm climate. We live in Los Angeles, where the weather never requires thermal underwear or après-ski anything.

So it's off to the ski shop we go to outfit ourselves for our snow country adventure. We hit the only ski shop in Beverly Hills. Big mistake. "Beverly Hills" should have been my first clue. I find some *adorable* jackets for my girls, who, at this time, are two-and-a-half and five years. The price tag: $175.00 each! I can't believe my eyes! That doesn't include ski pants, suspenders, hats, ear muffs, goggles, gloves, warmers for the gloves, ski socks, warmers for the ski socks, thermal underwear, scarves, lip balm, and after-ski boots. This will never do because we have to buy complete outfits for everyone: Tony, Alex, Ari, and me.

We all head for one of those huge sports places where things are spread all over what seems to be an acre. Everything is piled so high you need a scaffold to reach what you want. Inevitably, what you want is always in a box either at the very top of the stack, or it's the very last thing on the bottom. Nothing is ever in order according to size. We actually have to take a lunch break because it takes so darn long to find what we need.

After we pile everything into three shopping carts, we stand in a line of fellow shoppers that stretches down to the area that has the gym equipment. *No temptation there!*

Every time I go into one of these mega-stores, I always feel uncomfortable. They treat everyone like a criminal, as if we're all just waiting for the chance to steal something. There are so many security gadgets and tags on the items, it takes forever to find the price tag. Then, after you've made your purchase—and given them every form of identification imaginable—you head for the exit, only to be stopped by a guy who has been watching you. He has to check the items you bought against your receipts, just in case you managed somehow to sneak in a treadmill! Of course, he goes through each bag and every item. *I really* need *to scream!*

Once we get home, I have the pleasure of packing. I need two huge suitcases just for the ski clothes. I have to figure how many days we're going to be away (to calculate clean underwear, of course) and make sure the kids have enough proper just-hanging-around clothes. And, oh yes, I must find a winter coat for our dog, Pocket, a white teacup poodle who weighs only four pounds.

The big day arrives. We head for the airport for what should be a ninety-minute flight. That is, if you fly directly from L.A. to Sun Valley. But, of course, there are no direct flights, only L.A. to Salt Lake City for a three-hour layover before heading on to Sun Valley. Once we arrive in Salt Lake City, I pray that the weather will hold up so our flight won't be delayed.

Six hours later, we board the plane for a bumpy, turbulent ride over the mountains. The flight is diverted to Boise because of a blinding snowstorm. When we land in Boise, we board a *bus* for a four-and-a-half hour ride to Sun Valley. The whole trip so far has taken thirteen-and-a-half hours, and we've flown over one-fourth of the United States. Nonetheless, the minute you get off the plane and get a whiff of that pure mountain air, you instantly feel better. Of course, the feeling lasts only about thirty seconds because as soon as you take another deep breath, you realize you can't take three steps without having trouble breathing.

When you go from sea level to 9,000 feet, the altitude hits you like a ton of bricks. You spend the next week trying to adjust to the flu-like symptoms of altitude sickness: shortness of breath, dizziness, sleeplessness, disorientation, and on and on. The bus goes about twenty-eight miles an hour because there is, after all, a nasty snowstorm. We're finally near our destination when the bus driver makes a right turn and promptly loses control of the bus and slides into a huge snow bank. We are *so* stuck! I figure we are only a few hundred feet from the condo we've rented. Everyone is deathly silent, except me.

"Outta here!" I shout. "Can someone please open the hatch and we'll carry our luggage."

At this point, Alex takes Pocket outside so she can relieve herself. Poor thing was about to burst. After placing Pocket in the snow, she comes back to help us retrieve some luggage. But when she goes over to retrieve the dog, she's gone! Vanished. The snow is so deep and so white and Pocket is so tiny and white that we can't find her. The girls start to cry, and everyone gets off the bus to help find our lost little creature. Eventually, we find her in about two feet of snow, completely freaking out.

Now that Pocket is safe, I invite all of our fellow bus passengers to our condo—if they help us schlep our luggage off the bus and haul it home. We use the phone in the condo to call for help for the bus. I am left with thirty-seven strangers in my temporary house that has absolutely no food. I can't even offer anyone hot chocolate because there is nothing in the cupboards. I thought we would have arrived by 3:30, giving us plenty of time to get to the market and stock up on food and other goodies. I tell Tony I'm going to go to the market now to pick up a few things. "No, let's wait and all go together," he insists. So we all end up waiting until help comes for our newfound friends.

After they're all safely on their way, off we go to the market to pick up the bare essentials to get us through tonight and tomorrow morning. At the checkout counter, I notice that Arianna actually looks *green.* Without so much as one tiny warning, she simply opens her mouth and projectile vomits everywhere: all over the tabloids, candy, gum, countertops, and checkout person. I am horrified! The checkout person tells me not to worry. "It's only altitude sickness," she says, then gets on the loudspeaker and calmly says, "A. S. on check stand!"

They have a code name for this? Suddenly, out of nowhere, an attendant arrives with paper towels, a mop, and a bucket. He wipes everything, including Arianna, clean. I'm too stunned to speak.

We go back to our little house to bunk down for the night. I give the kids a hot bath and some warm chamomile tea and they're out. I head toward the stairs. Our bedroom is on the second floor. There are fourteen steps! It seems like *so* many! I can do this, I think, bounding up the stairs like a gazelle wearing lead weights. Upon reaching the top, I have to actually hang on to the wall while I catch my breath. But, I think, *At least this day is over and tomorrow we start our family ski vacation.*

I crawl into a huge, four-poster, king-size bed on which carved wooden bears attempt to eat each other. The bed is so high off the floor that I actually need a chair to climb into it. The down comforter is so gigantic I can barely lift it. I can't see Tony; he's disappeared into the comforter on his side of the bed. Once we're both snug as a bug, we just lie there staring at the ceiling trying to catch our breath. The altitude has kicked in, big-time.

Why didn't I remember? I can't sleep in high altitude! So I prepare for a *long* night of tossing and turning. As I lie there, I look out the window at the breathtaking scenery. The light of the full moon is illuminating the blue-black sky. There are so many bright stars that it looks like God has shaken confectioner's sugar all over the heavens. The tops of the mountains shimmer proudly with freshly fallen snow. You can sense what the air smells like and can almost feel that first burst in your lungs when you deeply inhale. I stare out the window for a very long time before drifting off into a twilight sleep until dawn.

When I awake, I try to get out of bed, but it takes some serious effort. I feel like I climbed every one of those mountains outside the window. Washing my face jolts me out of my stupor. The water is so cold that it shrinks the capillaries in my face and gives me an instant face-lift. I brush my teeth and immediately feel the nerves in my teeth pulsating and making my gums numb. I spit out the water, then take a drink to relieve my dry throat. I immediately get a brain freeze. I'm awake now!

The kids come stumbling down the stairs with hair stuck to their cheeks and mouths. The central heating must have stuffed up their noses, forcing them to breathe through their mouths. I guess their saliva just dried as it slid down their faces.

I send them off to wash up for breakfast. They also return with brain freezes. I have some medicine for that: a cup of hot chocolate. "Don't forget, you have to be in ski school by nine," I say.

Mistake One: Don't ever tell your kids they are going to school for *anything!* It's always met with shrill screams of rebellion. "No way!" they shriek in unison.

Alex is beside herself. "School?" she moans. "That's such a dumb idea! How could you ruin my vacation? The ski instructor is mean!"

"What do you mean, he's mean?" I ask. "You haven't even met him!" I stop myself. "You know what, we are not having this conversation," I say, pausing between sentences as I attempt to breathe in some oxygen. "You're going to ski school, and that's that! Hurry and get dressed. We have to hustle because we have to stop to rent skis."

Mistake Two: Never assume that kids know how to dress for snow.

"I'm not cold, and I'm not wearing that stupid jacket!" Alex informs me. "It makes me look like an igloo." She stops for a breath of oxygen, too. "And you can forget about the ski pants," she adds. "I'm wearing my jeans."

"You cannot wear your jeans to ski!" I reply. "They won't keep your legs from freezing, and if you fall and get them wet, you'll be miserable."

That's met with, "Oh, Mom, you're so old-fashioned."

"Old-fashioned?" I gasp. "What does that have to do with your legs freezing?"

By this time, Dad has joined in with his ever-ready solution.

"If you kids don't do what your mother has asked, then we're going to leave and go home," he says.

"Fine," they both chime in. "We're not wearing those stupid clothes!"

Turning to Mr. I'll-Take-Care-Of-This, I say, "Okay, Dr. Spock, now what?" I step forward with *all* the clothes and simply state, "If you don't put these clothes on right now, I'm going to kill you and pull your hair!"

The girls start laughing. They tell me how ridiculous it would be for me to pull out their hair *after* I kill them. Finally, they start to put on layer upon layer of clothing. It's 8:05 A.M. By 8:40 we are set to roll. And I do mean roll. By the time they get all of their clothing on, starting with the thermal underwear, they look like ticks ready to pop! I'm totally out of breath as I struggle to make sure their snow boots are on properly with no possibility of snow getting in.

They look like two tiny astronauts on their way to the car, tilting back and forth and from side to side. I'm so excited that they're dressed and heading for the car that I totally forget that *I* need to get dressed. I have to hurry because they're already complaining that they're too hot. They start to scream bloody murder because now they can't get the seat belt to go around them. Once they're buckled in, I feel sorry for them. They look like little stuffed sausages! All I can see are their sweet tiny faces, surrounded by mounds of insulation. I need to move *fast!* Off we go to the ski shop to rent our skis.

Of course, we can't find an empty space in the parking lot of the ski rental shop. And once we finally find a spot on the street, we can't get the door fully open because the snow plows left mounds of snow on the curb. As we squeeze through the car door and climb over the mounds, we all stand there looking at each other like we don't know what to do next. *That's because we don't!* We are so unaccustomed to breathing thin air that we actually go blank for a second, trying to figure out *why* we are standing on a sidewalk in a strange town. Finally, it hits us: ski rentals!

As we push our way down the street, I can't help but notice that this little town is truly charming. It looks like something from the turn of the century. Snow is gently falling, giving everything a Currier and Ives feel. You can almost sense the presence of the miners who settled here long before the arrival of the skiers. The streets are cobblestone and the buildings are the original brick. Yes, the bank is now a trendy restaurant and the old feed stores are packed with pricey cashmere, china, and jewelry., but the hitching posts are still intact. It almost makes you wish you had a horse.

Finally, we get to the rental shop. When we open the door, we're hit with a blast of hot air from the heaters. Immediately, the kids begin whining. "Mom, it's too hot!"

"Don't worry," I say. "We're going to be out of here in no time. So don't take anything off."

"Oh, yeah?" says Alexandra. She's pointing toward the ski rack, where there's a line of skiers waiting to rent skis. A collective moan rises from all of us. Tony assures us that he'll take care of everything. "Just be patient," he says.

As Tony stands in line, the kids start to walk around the shop looking at all the merchandise. I also start to walk around and notice items that look familiar to me: hats with the initials A.T. laying on the display case in the goggles and sunglass department; a little color-coordinated left glove on the floor; a tiny scarf and another left glove and two jackets that shouldn't be in the sweater area. I look around for my kids, only to discover they are completely undressed down to their corduroys and turtlenecks. They have also managed to jiggle out of their boots (haven't seen those anywhere)—and are running around in their wooly stockings soaking up the moisture from the snow dragged in from the street.

Tony somehow manages to get someone to help us quickly. He calls me over with the kids and introduces us all to some guy named Sven. He's the color of red shoe leather. He greets us with a blindingly white smile and the bluest eyes that peek through reddish eyelashes.

I'm surprised at the amount of paperwork you have to complete before they will even fit you for skis. After Sven explains that they're not responsible for the death of your children or any part of you that breaks, he cheerily goes into the back of the shop and fetches a pair of what will turn out to be many pairs of skis that may or may not fit you. Of course, before he can fit the skis, he must fit the ski boot.

When I take my kids shoe shopping, I always make a point to make sure the shoes don't hurt and aren't too tight. But ski boots are supposed to fit tight and feel snug. So no matter what boot we put on the girls, they complain. "We're dying!" they scream. "It's too tight. I can't wear it!"

Finally, we find the perfect fit, and Tony and his new buddy Sven try to explain to the girls why they're leaning forward at an odd angle and can't actually walk. I head off to find their missing pieces of clothing and pray no one has actually purchased any of them. I'm so friggin' hot and exhausted at this point that I just grab all the gear, including all the clothes, stuff it in a bag, and head for the car. As I open the door to leave, a blast of cold air brings me out of my stupor and I make a beeline for the car. I turn around and wait for the kids to catch up. Their ski boots are so heavy they thump and drag their feet as they try to get to the car. They try to crawl in, but I have to hoist them up because they can't lift their heavy ski boots themselves.

Finally, we're ready to ski! We arrive at the lift. There is no parking anywhere remotely near the entrance. So Tony drops us off, telling us to wait. It's cold, so we head for the lodge. Once we get in the lodge, there are people standing in line again. You have to register your kids if you're going to put them in ski school. Kids are screaming everywhere. (*I can do this*, I repeat to myself.) I head for the back of the line as I listen to my kids saying what all of the other kids seem to be saying, "No way we're gonna go!"

By now, Arianna is on the floor having a tantrum, rolling around like a beach ball. She has so many layers on that she looks like a sumo wrestler who has fallen and can't get up! I act like I don't know her. Tony finally arrives and starts to complain about how much the lessons cost.

"All right then, Tony, what do you suggest we do, take the kids up ourselves?" I ask.

He realizes that we aren't equipped to teach the kids, so he has to bite the bullet. When we reach the front of the line, more paperwork is placed in front of us to remind us that the ski company is not responsible if any of us die, break something, or are caught in an avalanche. Good Lord! The kids are now both crying because they don't want to be caught in an avalanche, and, more importantly, they don't know anyone in their class. "We want to go home to L.A.!" they say.

Tony and I remain firm in our commitment to the ultimate ski vacation. Off we go, leaving our kids screaming for us, their pleas of "Don't leave me!" resonating in our ears.

We have every intention to ski with the kids in a few days, once they get a few runs under their belts. But for now, the two of us head off to the bigger mountain to do some skiing by ourselves. Of course, it's nothing like the ski poster. We get to the other lodge and wait in another long line for lift tickets. This time, it's me who's griping about the high price of lift tickets. As they stick my ticket to my zipper, I turn to pick up my skis. I hoist them over my shoulder and head toward the gondola that will hoist us into the heavens. As I'm walking to the lift, I'm acutely aware of how difficult it is to walk with boots that only Frankenstein could manage. I have to stop every few seconds to catch my breath.

As we ride skyward, I'm trying to make sense of all this: Let's see . . . we've spent all this time and all this money to find a place to stay and purchase clothes that can't ever possibly fit into our closets once we get back home. My kids hate me. We've stood in lines to rent ski boots and skis, then the endless line for tickets to the ski lift. Let's not forget the line for food and hot chocolate. Then, there's another line to go up the ski lift so you can freeze your ass off as you take it to the top of the mountain!

Once I reach the top, I *always* fall as I get off of the gondola. They *always* have to stop the chair lift to untangle me. And everyone *always* watches as I try to regain my composure while struggling to stand up. I can never quite figure out how to actually do it gracefully. Forget gracefully. How to get up at all! The young guys running the lift come over to me and lift me up, gripping under my arms until I'm balanced. I pretend like it's no big deal. Once they get to know me, they just stop the chairs when they see me preparing to disembark/fall. That way, they can simply come and get me.

Atop the mountain, I look down at the majestic vista before me and I finally get it. The snow-covered mountains are utterly breath-taking. The sky is a cold, steely gray. I feel as if I could ski right into it and keep going forever. This is it! This is the reason I've put up with everything. Tomorrow, I vow, I'll return with my kids and share this wondrous moment with them.

This is the stuff that those ski vacation posters are made of, and I'm eager to become one with the fantasy. Tony starts down the mountain and I admire his form. He so effortlessly glides from one side to the other. I gently push off to follow him. I make my first turn, lose my balance, and tumble down the mountain, gaining speed as I fall. My one-piece ski suit creates absolutely no friction between the snow and me whatsoever. I, too, am gliding down the mountain—*on my back!* I finally stop halfway down the slope, and when I sit up and look around, I realize I'm missing not one but both of my skis. Some nice boys find them and bring them to me. "Hey, lady, you don't look so good," they say. "Should we call the ski patrol?"

Now I'm thinking, *How many more days are left?* It's amazing. Vacation mishaps are like labor pains. You know it's going to hurt, but you can't seem to remember the pain.

Well, let's just say that I managed to survive the ski trip to Idaho, but I still hadn't learned my lesson. Instead, we turned our attention to the always-popular theme parks that dot the country. After all, I reasoned, where else but in a park decked out as a magical place could we have a fairy-tale vacation?

—— ⚜ ——

Always searching for new and exciting things to enjoy as a family, we soon find ourselves in an endless line of theme parks. We try all of them, but the theme parks that drive me closest to insanity are the water theme parks.

Everything smells like suntan lotion, chlorine, and sweat. As I watch my kids float by me in enormous inner tubes, I'm polarized by the thought of all those kids peeing in the water. One time everyone had to leave the water immediately because the lifeguards informed us they'd found a "floatie." And I don't mean the ones you put on your arms to keep you afloat.

It seems that every time a floatie rises, you have to evacuate so they can drain the enormous pool and fill it up again. Ugh! Having tried this water thing once, I vow never to return. I'll try land instead.

The next summer, we decide to go to Florida. The only thing is, I'd forgotten how unbearably *hot* Florida is in July! Why would anyone even consider going in July? Well, the kids' school year doesn't end until the middle of June. And airlines and hotels offer unbelievable rates for flights and rooms in July. No wonder. No one in his or her right mind goes to Florida in the middle of summer. That's why they offer great airline prices, hotel rooms, free kids' meals, and a coupon for ice cream!

The second we get off the plane, my body temperature shoots up ten degrees. It's like the blast you get when you open your oven door to baste a turkey. As we walk on the tarmac to the terminal, I can see the heat rising. The air actually looks wavy.

Once inside, I announce to my family, "I'm not leaving the building to go outside again until we leave to go home."

They all shoot me the "Mom-don't-start" look. "Okay troops," I say, rallying. "Let's do this." Off we go to check into the hotel.

I decide to apply a battle strategy to the trip, believing that if we get up early, we can beat the heat of the middle of the day. But it doesn't matter. Dawn in Florida in mid-summer begins at eighty-eight degrees. In the shade. The humidity is 1,000 percent, or at least it seems that way. By mid-afternoon, I feel like The Wicked Witch of the West: *I'm melting, I'm melting!*

We find a bench under a tree and sit in the shade with our seventeenth iced drink. We watch all of the armies of sun-worshipping families strolling by. You've seen them: the people walking around with hot reddish-pink arms and legs jutting out of their sleeveless shirts and cut-off shorts. I always want to run over to them and say: "Oh my God, do know how red your arms are? You know you're really going to feel it tonight. Maybe you should put on some sunscreen, or maybe get out of the sun!" Their kids, who are riding in tandem in strollers, are literally hanging over the sides, completely lifeless. I want to save them all! Tony would always tell me to "mind my own business."

As we sit there on the bench, we watch the cartoons come to life as assorted theme park characters stroll by us. I marvel that they can survive in their suffocating woolen suits. How can they breathe? It is just so darned *hot!* Maybe I should go over there and offer some cold water. Again, Tony says, "Mind your own business." As I contemplate whether or not to intercede, the main character, with his wide happy grin and huge ears, whom everyone has gathered around, begins to wobble. He takes a few doddering steps and faints dead away!

I spring into action, running over to him and trying to pull his costumed head off so he can get some air. This is met with a cry from the throng of children and adults gathered near, "No-o-o-o-o-o-o-o-o!" Out of nowhere, eight employees appear, all holding notebooks. They scream "No!" to me, then start to speak into pins on their lapels. (*Who are they talking to, 007?*)

"What do you mean, no?" I yell back. I am firmly reprimanded by the guy wearing the biggest pin. "Miss," he barks in a tone that makes it clear he means business, "under no circumstances are you to remove his head!"

"Why not?" I demand.

"Because if you remove his head in front of the other guests, you may traumatize some child!" says Mr. Big Pin.

"Are you nuts? There's a *human being* in there! Who cares if it traumatizes some kid? They'll end up in therapy someday anyway!" I scream.

Well, Mr. Big Pin will hear none of this. He and the rest of his pin-wearing friends simply surround this huge, grinning rodent and carry him behind ominous-looking gates that are bedecked with signs that warn "DO NOT ENTER UNDER ANY CONDITIONS!" It makes you wonder what goes on back there.

No sooner do they shut the gate than the same cartoon character (surely with someone new inside) is back out in the park, shaking hands and taking pictures with children. I never do find out what happened to the *human* in the suit.

I swear those theme parks are like communist countries. You are not individuals. You are a number, and your name is "Guest." You must conform to their way of running things, or you don't do well under the circumstances. You stand in line for *everything*, and you stand there for a very long time. It always completely boggles my mind why anyone would stand in line for over an hour for a ride that lasts *three minutes*. The kids hang on to me, complaining that they're either tired, hungry, bored, hot (always hot), or "Have to pee." And every year, we do it again. Why?

Memories that will stay in your heart are real, very real. Advertisers know they have an eager audience when they market your vacation as a storybook experience. But the fact that your vacations never turn out like the brochures shouldn't deter you from packing up your bags and trying it all again next year. The challenge here is not to set yourself up for a fall. You need to take the extra time and effort to plan for things that may and will go wrong. Kids are ornery and moody little characters who sometimes can get to the best of us. But I love my kids, and even though our vacations don't turn out exactly like the brochures, I wouldn't miss all these wonderful memories for the world.

The calm before the storm of teenage rebellion.
Tony, Zach, me, Alex, and Kathryn.

CHAPTER 8

Raising Teenagers

"WOW, Zach and Kathryn look really different in this picture," Arianna exclaims. She holds out a photo of her stepbrother and stepsister as teenagers.

As the first children to enter my life, Zach and Kathryn held a special place in the fairy tale I believed I would live as a mom. This was probably one of the reasons I failed to see that they were in trouble as teenagers. I wanted to believe in the fairy tale. The reality was, as always, very different.

I used to think I was my mother's favorite until I had children of my own. That's when I realized moms don't have favorites. We love our children equally, with the same intensity, and when it comes to kids, everything is intense. Raising mine, I've experienced incredible highs and heart-wrenching lows.

As time has gone on, I've come to realize that my children aren't really mine. They don't belong to me. They are a gift given to me for a while, a very short while. During our brief time with our children, it is our privilege as parents to love them unconditionally and to guide and nurture them, physically and spiritually. It is a responsibility that sometimes overwhelms and frightens me.

Something happens when kids reach puberty. I can only surmise it is God's way of starting the separation process. Our children want to break away from the safety of the nest and start out on their own, as they should. But the process is neither pretty nor smooth. Teenagers do things that get you so frustrated and upset that you get to a point where you actually can't wait until they're able to be out on their own!

There are so many things you need to keep on top of, and frankly, parenting teenagers is exhausting. You have to watch over the type of friends they hang out with, and pray that you've taught them enough that they'll make the right choices when confronted with temptations to have sex, smoke cigarettes, drink alcohol, or do drugs. You think you're doing a great job until you get that phone call in the middle of the night. Nothing, and I mean *nothing*, is worse than that dreaded phone call.

—— ⚹ ——

The shrill ring of the telephone jolted me out of a deep sleep. *This can't be good.* I knew that any post-midnight call was never someone calling to chat. I didn't have friends in Europe wanting to wish me a good morning. As I reached over to pick up the phone, my heart was in the pit of my stomach, and I could feel the adrenaline coursing through my body. I broke into a cold sweat. The minute the unfamiliar voice on the other end began to speak, I held my breath.

Tony bolted up and asked, "What's wrong? What's wrong?" so loudly that I couldn't make out what the woman on the other end was saying. I waved frantically for him to be quiet, then sent up a quick prayer, silently pleading that no one was dead. The caller was the mother of a friend of my then fourteen-year-old daughter, Kathryn, who was sleeping over at their house.

"Get over here quick," the mother blurted out. "Kathryn is in and out of consciousness, incoherent, and vomiting *everywhere.*"

I tried to remain as calm as possible. "Does she have a fever?" I asked the mother. "Did she eat anything that might not agree with her? Do you think she might be coming down with something?"

It never occurred to me to ask if she had been drinking or doing drugs. I knew I could trust my daughter. She would *never* have done anything like that. Furthermore, I had been a responsible parent and had made sure the sleepover would be properly supervised.

The reply from the other end shocked me. "I don't know what happened," she said, "because I haven't been home."

"Excuse me?" I asked incredulously. "You weren't home? What do you mean you weren't home? Are you the same person I spoke to *twice* to make sure you were going to be there with the kids? You have eight teenagers at your house, including visiting boys, and you're telling me you weren't home? Where were you?"

She said that she and her husband decided to go out for a "quick bite" around 10:30. Apparently, while they were out, her daughter found the keys to the liquor cabinet. My fear turned into anger, then rage. Tony said I needed to calm down and deal with the fact that Kathryn could be in real trouble. We should take care of that issue first. "We'll be over in twenty minutes," I told the absentee mom.

The ride was torture. We caught every red light, and it seemed to take forever to get there. When we finally arrived at the giant housing complex, all of the apartments looked exactly the same. I couldn't tell the difference between one apartment and the next. It felt like a very bad nightmare. I stood in the middle of a courtyard, shivering in the cold, wondering which bell to ring. Suddenly, I heard Kathryn's voice. She was moaning and speaking gibberish, extremely loudly. I got my bearings and realized that she was in the apartment directly behind me.

When we arrived, the parents couldn't even look me in the eye. I said nothing to them. The smell of alcohol was so overpowering that it nauseated me. Kathryn was lying on the floor in the fetal position, talking to herself and making no sense.

"Have you taken any pills along with the alcohol?" I asked.

She couldn't answer. I lifted her off the floor, and we carried her to the car. We went straight to the emergency room to have her stomach pumped. I had no idea what she'd consumed, and I wasn't going to take any chances. She kept trying to fall asleep in my arms. I was frightened that if I let her sleep, she would never regain consciousness. I spoke to her the whole way and forced her to stay awake.

The emergency room attendants accepted her immediately. Tony stayed at the reception area to handle the paperwork while the hospital staffers whisked Kathryn away down the corridor. I stood and watched my daughter's motionless body being wheeled away from me. Her face was ghostly pale. My knees began to buckle, and I wanted to scream. I was trembling; I couldn't speak or move. A nurse finally came over and brought me back to Tony. We sat in the waiting room for two hours, alone in the middle of the night.

Finally, after what seemed like an eternity, a doctor came and announced that Kathryn was going to be just fine. I exhaled for the first time that night. He said that she had alcohol poisoning.

"What's that?" I asked.

He explained that alcohol poisoning is what happens to a person who has had more to drink then her body can tolerate. Kathryn had consumed too much booze in a very short period of time. He also told us he found no evidence of any drugs. They had pumped her stomach, and now she would have to sleep it off and endure a very bad hangover.

The doctor held my hand between his two hands and gently

squeezed. He tapped the top of my hand twice, indicating to me he understood how I was feeling.

I wondered if he knew how angry I was and that I could barely contain my emotions. I was relieved and grateful that Kathryn was going to be all right. But I was really angry at those irresponsible parents and at Kathryn's breach of confidence, and I resented the guilt that I felt for not being able to protect my child. I know that I had no control over what happened that night, but I was still angry.

A nurse asked if I wanted to spend the night with Kathryn. "Absolutely!" I said. She told me that a room would be available soon.

In the meantime, Kathryn was lying on a cot in a tiny holding room. I walked into the darkened space. She was out cold, but breathing normally. She seemed so peaceful. I instinctively placed my hand on her forehead. Her temperature seemed fine. I pushed aside some stray strands of hair from her face and gently kissed her as I pulled the covers over her shoulders. As I did this, I realized that I left her feet exposed. At five feet, eleven inches she was too tall for the blankets, so I got another one to cover her feet.

As I did that, I noticed a tiny incubator in the corner of the room. Looking at that incubator, and then at my daughter, I remembered as if it were yesterday the first week of her life. I remembered staring through the nursery glass for hours, vowing that nothing was ever going to hurt my baby. I broke down and started to sob.

After giving birth and getting handed your first baby, you can hardly see him or her through your tears; you are so joyful and at peace with the world. When you hold your child in your arms for the very first time, the feeling is indescribable. The instinct to protect is overwhelming. *No one will ever hurt my child!* You vow that you will always be there for your son or daughter no matter what happens.

As you stare down at your baby's tiny, delicate face, you of course never think, "Gee, I wonder how I can screw up your life?" No, you vow that you will give your child the best life ever, and that you will have the best relationship ever. For the most part, you do. Then, she turns into a teenager.

The next morning, Kathryn and I left the hospital, shaken but relieved that everything was going to be all right. This time. But it was only the first of many trials with my kids.

— ⚘ —

I honestly believe that if women gave birth to teenagers, no one would have children. What a roller coaster ride.

I loved each and every stage my children went through, except for the teen years. I'm being honest. When they're babies, they depend on you for everything. You can hold, kiss, and cuddle them, and you're able to dress them any way you want. They think you're the best thing since breast milk. That doesn't last very long. Soon they start asserting their independence—perhaps in anticipation of the teenage battles that are to come.

I used to love to dress Zach in navy blue shorts with a polo shirt and a sweater vest. He looked so adorable in his knee socks and saddle shoes. That lasted until he was two, at which point he would roll around on the floor, absolutely refusing to get dressed. He hated everything I presented. He wanted to pick out his outfit on his own, and it was always the same T-shirt and pair of long pants every day, all day long.

My girls were worse. Kathryn would wear only sundresses. We lived in New York at the time, and she insisted on a sundress even when it was barely sixteen degrees outside. I tried to explain that she needed to wear something warm, but she didn't care. She wouldn't wear anything I suggested. No sweaters, not even a warm wool skirt. I tried giving her a choice between two weather-appropriate outfits;

she hated both of them. It was a battle every day just to get her dressed, and I dreaded it.

On the other hand, when Alex was two, she would wear only jeans, sneakers, and tie-dyed shirts. This was the 1980s; the 1960s were long gone. She would draw tattoos on her stomach and arms and would be proud to show her dad her latest creation. The tattoos made Tony crazy. Where did she get these ideas? It turns out they were just shades of teenaged things to come.

Arianna wanted to wear only bathing suits with matching headbands and flip-flops, regardless of where she was headed for the day. It took me forever to get her dressed. After a while, I learned to pick and choose my battles.

As she and Alex grew, they only became more opinionated. By the time they were teenagers, I was worn out. I was tired of arguing.

Just when I thought things were going well in the wardrobe department, Britney Spears burst on the scene and ruined everything. She made her fashion statement by wearing jeans that barely covered her pubic hair, skimpy tops that stopped way north of her belly button, and a matching boa constrictor (a real one) to top it all off. At the time, Britney claimed she was a pure and innocent virgin, but she sure didn't dress like one. This was absolutely *not* how I wanted my girls to dress to go to the movies or the mall or . . . *anywhere!* I had to put my foot down.

In response, they whined that I was too "old-fashioned" and a "total embarrassment." They complained that I "knew nothing" and was "ruining their lives." Big surprise.

You can't imagine the concoctions they came up with. They looked like they came straight from the audience of *The Jerry Springer Show.* I tried to be supportive and give them positive feedback on their wardrobe choices, but I had reached my limits. I couldn't let them leave the house looking like that.

I've discovered that girls start to test the waters when they're around eleven, but are mostly manageable until they actually hit puberty. When that happens, you find yourself wondering, "Who are these people, and why are they so angry?"

Watching my kids go through puberty and become teenagers has made me wonder about a lot of things. When they were very young, they really looked up to their father and me. How many times did I have to drop everything, just to praise a cartwheel? How many times did I respond to, "Hey, Mom! Watch this dive!" They used to look to us for approval and praise, and they took such delight in seeing our excitement over their tiniest accomplishments. What happened to their perception of us when they became adolescents?

I think I know what it is. It's a phenomenon I've dubbed *parent-tinnitus*. You've probably heard of tinnitus, a ringing or roaring sound in the ear that can be heard only by the affected person. On the other hand, with "parent-tinnitus," your teenager will hear a ringing in his ears (your voice), but he will also have an uncanny ability *not* to hear it. This condition starts to rear its ugly head when your child is approaching twelve; by the time she or he turns thirteen, you're considered an aged moron. Everything you say and do is out of date, completely unrealistic, and—most of all—embarrassing. My favorite is when my daughters tell me, "You know *nothing* about fashion!" I must have wasted those twenty years I spent as a high-fashion model. What could I possibly know about *today's* fashions?

—— ⚘ ——

It sounds clichéd, but it's true: Before you know it, your kids go from watching Saturday morning cartoons to sitting forever in front of their computers. I understand the allure of cartoons, but can anyone explain to me the obsession with "talking" online? Why can't they just pick up the phone? It's so much faster and easier. I'm completely out of the loop. What's the allure?

My daughter Alex tried to explain it all to me. She spoke in slow, exaggerated words, mouthing each one carefully and loudly like I was from some foreign country. I told her to quit patronizing me!

I'm concerned about chat rooms, and the language they use horrifies me. I've seen how some of these kids write online to each other. To make matters worse, extremely graphic pornography ads pop up all the time. No matter how worldly they think they are, my kids are just not ready to handle *that*. We have a block on the computer, but I know it doesn't work one hundred percent. Who knows what's getting past it when I'm not there? I've talked to my daughters about the danger of corresponding with people they don't know. Every time, I get a dismissive sigh telling me they "know how to handle the situation." How can they know? They're just children. Even *I* don't know how to deal with it! I used to worry when they would go out. Now, I worry about them in our own home.

If only there were some books I could buy that would explain the truth about parenting teenagers. Here are some titles I could use:

Who Are You, and What Have You Done with My Child?
"M.O.M." Mom or Moron: Which Are You?
Get Out of My Room! I Hate You! But Before You Go, Will You
　　Take Me and Two Friends to the Galleria?
Pierce Your Nose and Pierce My Heart
How to Enforce a Curfew without Losing Your Dignity
Deciphering Screen Names
How to Survive the Teenage Years with Your Marriage Intact

Obviously, these titles are not real books. I did read plenty of books on raising kids, but nothing I read prepared me for what really happened. I ended up just trying to listen to my heart and saying and doing what I thought was right.

Here are a few things I did:

1. Talked to my kids openly and honestly about sex. *They were grossed out!*
2. Told them about the hazards of cigarette smoking.
3. Warned them about alcohol abuse.
4. Spoke to them about the dangers of drugs.
5. Stressed the importance of a good education.
6. Made them understand that not going to college was not an option.
7. Talked to them about safe sex and reminded them of dear friends who are no longer with us because of AIDS.
8. Reassured them that they could talk to their father and me about anything, and we would understand and be open-minded. (I get the feeling Alex and Arianna don't believe me, and honestly I don't know how open-minded I'm really going to be. I didn't do so well the first time. I'll try, though.)
9. Encouraged celibacy. We told them not to be embarrassed to be a virgin, even if their friends were not.
10. Spoke to them about waiting to get married to have sex. This is the way we brought them up. Is it realistic to think they'll wait? To be honest, I'm not so sure. I must be real here. We told them that we realize we're living in a real world with real temptations, and waiting to have sex until after they get married is a choice that they—and they alone—must make when the time comes. In the meantime, all we can do is to prepare them spiritually and emotionally, and let them know that no matter what happens, we will always be there and not pass judgment.

11. Told them that if there does come a time when they give in and have sex, they need to use condoms. Safe sex, safe sex, safe sex.
12. Reassured them that God would never abandon them, and neither would we.

I have always tried to keep the lines of communication open for every moment of my children's lives. I want them to know that I will always be there for them, and that they can always talk to me about *anything.* How, then, have they sometimes slipped through the cracks of parental control? All I have to do is remember what it was like to be a teenager. I was a good kid, but I managed to slip quite a few things past old Mom and Dad.

As a parent, you love your children so unconditionally that the idea of them doing anything stupid seems completely unimaginable. Even if you did those same things yourself as a teenager, you refuse to believe that your children would make the same mistakes. But by denying your children's problems, you only delay how quickly you can get help for them.

—— ✳ ——

I had a rude awakening when I discovered that my son Zachary was in real trouble. With all of the information available about the warning signs of drug abuse, you'd think I would have recognized it. But I never saw them—or I wanted to ignore them. By denying the obvious, I avoided having to face the difficult reality. I was too proud to admit there was a problem. *There was no way my baby would do something as stupid as drugs!* I trusted him and thought that the lines of communication were wide open.

It started innocently enough. Zach came home from school with some friends. He didn't seem very coherent, and when he got out of the car, he vomited all over the front lawn. I thought he was coming down with the flu. "What's wrong, honey?" I asked.

"Oh Mom, I did something stupid," he said. "I smoked a cigarette. It really made me sick, and I need to go lie down. I feel awful. I'll never do *that* again!"

I felt good that he was being honest with me. I thought I had won a victory! I was so sure that he had learned his lesson about tobacco that he would never smoke again.

Believe it or not, I actually said, "Well, let this serve as a lesson for you. I'm sure you're sorry, and I know you're not feeling too great. Poor sweetie, come on. Mommy is going to make it better."

He gave me that Ferris Bueller look: the one where the slick kid looks like a sick, adorable puppy who's done nothing wrong. I put my arms around him and told him not to worry. I had him lie down, and I brought him a cold compress for his head.

Not only did he lie to me about this being his first time smoking, he omitted the fact that he was also high on grass. I found out about that later. Stupid me, I really thought it was the cigarettes that made him so sick.

I think the divine hand of God made me finally sit up and take notice. A few months later, Zach went to New York to visit his father. The rest of us—Tony, Kathryn, and young Alexandra and Arianna—were in Hawaii on vacation. The first morning we were there, I got everyone up and dressed. Tony went downstairs with the kids to wait in line for breakfast while I got myself ready for the day. Finally, I had some time alone. As I sat on the end of the bed, I stopped and paid attention to the television that had been on all morning. The familiar sound of the theme song to *Sesame Street* came on, and it made me smile. I took the remote and, in the process of flipping channels, I landed on one of the early morning talk shows.

"When we come back, a sixteen-year-old in seemingly great health collapses and dies," proclaimed the television announcer. "Find out why. We'll talk to his parents."

I didn't move for the whole two minutes while I waited for the commercials to end. The segment started with a picture of a great-looking sixteen-year-old boy. He looked like the picture of health, only now he was dead.

As the parents told their story, I had an out-of-body experience. While I was watching the TV, the mother on the screen became me. What she was saying and describing was exactly what I was going through with Zach, only her son was dead.

These parents were also involved in their son's life. But they never realized that he had a drug problem until it was too late. He collapsed during gym class while playing basketball. The paramedics arrived too late to save him. His heart stopped due to a mixture of pain pills and cocaine he had taken before class.

The television announcer said the boy had a major cocaine problem. He had been using for a while. The parents were completely unaware. How could they be so oblivious? Remember, there's the denial factor. You want to believe that you're being a great parent. You don't want to face the possibility that your child isn't following your lead. Denial seems like a comforting retreat, but in the end, it gets you nowhere.

The show's host asked the parents to give viewers a list of warning signs they should be watching for. As they talked about each warning sign, I realized that they could have been talking about my son. They described each and every one of Zach's symptoms. The list included grades slipping dramatically, failure to turn in homework, wanting to spend more time alone, excessive sleeping, refusing to eat and losing weight, lying, stealing, and becoming argumentative, manipulative, confrontational, and paranoid.

I called my son immediately. Without so much as a "hello," I launched into what I knew I had to say.

"Zach, this is Mom," I said, taking a deep breath before forging ahead. "I know you've been using drugs. I know you need help. I feel it's extremely urgent to get you into drug rehab as soon as possible." I waited.

"Mom," he said, finally, "I want to go." My heart sank. I was taken completely off guard. I wanted him to say, "You're wrong, Mom, I'm fine. You can test me. I'm fine."

"All right, honey," I said. "I need to do some research. I'll call you back."

I had no idea where to start. I didn't even know what kind of drugs he was on, or how bad off he was. *How could I not know?* I started pacing back and forth. *What am I going to do now?*

I quickly got dressed and found Tony and told him what had just happened. I was scared, anxious, and angry. How could this have happened right under our noses? *How can he be so bad off that he actually needs drug rehab?*

Tony and I got on it immediately. Our first call was to our family doctor. I also called Zach to find out exactly how bad off he was, what he had been using, and for how long. His answers shocked me: He'd been using for quite a while, and the list of drugs was long, wide, and deep. This was big time, and we needed big-time help.

When we got home from Hawaii, we continued researching doctors and clinics around the country. We decided to send him to a hard-core place in Minnesota to scare him straight. It was one of the toughest things I ever had to do in my life. I was devastated.

But when did this become about me, anyway? It was Zach who needed help in overcoming his addiction. Nevertheless, our whole family had a part in it, and we needed to stop denying the existence of the problem and face it head on. During rehabilitation, parents and the other siblings are required to go through therapy as well.

As this nightmare unfolded, I thought back to Zach's childhood. It seemed like it was only yesterday when he was on his way to his first day of kindergarten. I walked him to school, holding his hand tightly. As we stood in front of the huge school building, a teacher came out to greet us. She reached out her hand to escort Zach, and I remember looking down at our two joined hands. I watched as my grip loosened and he let go. I made a conscious effort to remember that moment, because it signified that he was starting a new chapter in his life. Letting go to venture to another place that didn't include me for the first time was a significant rite of passage. Zach was on his way. I prayed for all things wonderful and good in his life. I was so glad to be with him that day.

I wasn't there the day he checked into rehab. I couldn't hold his hand this time. No parents allowed. In fact, they didn't allow us to have contact with him for three whole weeks. They even coached us on exactly how to speak to Zach after the three-week period was over. We were given instructions that we had to follow *exactly*. If we failed, he would be expelled from the program. Under no circumstances was I allowed to tell him he could come home. No matter how much he cried or promised to be good, I was required to tell him to stay right where he was.

Drug abusers are excellent at the art of manipulation, and they'll say anything to get out of a tough situation. They're even more manipulative when they know that the other party is weak, and I was very weak. I worried about Zach constantly.

Rehab is tough. Once the addict arrives, he or she realizes that the rehab center is no cakewalk. There are very strict rules, and they must be followed to the letter. The two worst parts for the addict are the lack of access to drugs of any kind, and the fact that withdrawal is extremely painful.

I wasn't prepared for the first telephone call. I thought I would be strong. The moment I heard his shaky voice, I broke down and cried. I wanted him home. He did cry, and he did promise to be good, and I did believe him. My heart was telling me to bring him home; my instincts were telling me he needed to stay. In the end, he did stay. He stayed for nine long months.

During that time, Tony, John, Kathryn, and I went to see him three times. Each time was really tough. Each time I left, it tore at the core of my being. I blamed myself and felt it was entirely my fault. *How could I have let this happen?*

Listening to him in the Family Encounters group left me devastated. I had no idea of the depth of his emotions. He was angry about what had happened to his father with the cocaine allegations. He was angry over the divorce. He was angry over my remarriage. He was angry about school. He was angry at his friends. I thought I had covered all those bases with him with open discussions. Evidently, I had barely scratched the surface, and it was not nearly enough to help him through his struggle.

The turning point came at one of our last meetings. I broke down and openly blamed myself for everything. My son reached over to me, took my hand, and said, "Mom, this is not about you. You didn't make me smoke the dope. You didn't blow coke up my nose. You didn't put a needle in my arm. These were *my* choices. I did all of this. I'm responsible. I'm sorry I put you and Dad and the family through all this. Thanks for sticking by me." I sat there, unable to speak.

Oh my, what do I do with that information? Zach was releasing me from my guilt. I needed to trust that he meant what he said. Could I give him the benefit of the doubt? Could I ever trust him again? I would have to trust him in order for him to have control over his own life. Right then and there, I knew he was going to be all right.

I had no idea of the extraordinary courage it takes to make it through one of those programs and emerge a hero. I say "hero" because it takes a hero to face all of the demons that are part of the hideous diseases of alcohol and drug addiction, and to overcome them and release yourself from their grasp.

During our family encounter groups, we sat with twelve other families and shared the most intimate details with one another. We were told that nine of our kids would be repeaters of the program, that one would die of an overdose, and that only two would make it.

I never dreamed that my boy would grow up to be an addict. I thought he was going to go to some Ivy League school and get a job in a major investment firm. I was sure that he would marry a great woman and have three kids and live a great life. That was my fantasy.

The reality is that he turned to drugs and alcohol to deal with his problems. The reality is that he had problems. Before all of this happened, I couldn't fathom that he had any problems. What kind of problems can a fifteen-year-old have? He had parents who loved him. He went to a great school. He had his every need met. He was surrounded by a supportive, loving, closely-knit family.

I was so naïve. I believed that providing my version of a happy home would be sufficient to protect him from life's troubles. Who knew it could get so dark? The reality is that Zach will have to deal with his addiction every day for the rest of his life. The other reality is that he is one of the two who made it.

Today, Zach is doing exactly what he wants to be doing. He's a climber. Not a social climber; he's a mountain climber. He loves to be outdoors, teaching kids how to climb. He wants to have his own climbing gym, which he dreams of eventually expanding into a chain. He's a wonderful, sweet, and powerful man. I have enormous respect for him and for what he has been through. He's been clean and sober for sixteen years and takes it one day at a time.

He is my hero.

Spending time with my three daughters, Alex, Ari, and Kathryn.
Each is unique, and each is very special.

CHAPTER 9

Setting Boundaries and Letting Go

A S WE SORT THROUGH our boxes of memories, a photo rises from the bottomless stacks like a postcard from a rough journey. It's of my daughter, Kathryn, and me.

Though we're smiling in the photo, the picture takes me back to the period that bursts the fairy-tale bubble every time: The Raging Teenaged Hormone Zone.

I thought it was tough with a boy, but when a teenaged girl hits puberty, it's downright frightening. The mood swings are totally unpredictable, and you don't recognize the person who has been living in your house for the previous twelve years.

No matter what I said or did, I was a total idiot to Kathryn. I knew "nothing about life." I never understood "what it's like being a kid." The words my mother used to say—the very same ones I swore I would never use on my own kids—now emerged from my mouth on a daily basis: "You're not leaving the house looking like that, are you?" or "I need to talk to the parents first to make sure they'll be home" or even "You want to pierce your *what?* You do that and you're grounded forever!" And the old standby answer to each and every request: "No."

Right on cue, she responded with the very same replies that I remember from my own childhood: "You don't trust me" and, most popular of all, "I hate you!" The latter reply never worked for me because my grandmother would bop me on the head and yell, "Don't talk to your mother that way!" When I was growing up, I swore that I was going to trust my child, and that I would never make the same mistakes my parents made with me. I was going to be a *cool* parent.

I tried being a cool parent with Kathryn, and, boy, was *that* a big mistake. I only ended up enabling her. I now realize, after endless years of therapy, tears, and heartache, that giving in to my children's demands was the worst thing I could have done. I shouldn't have been afraid of setting boundaries. I learned that lesson the hard way.

I'm going to make this short and bittersweet. I gave in to all of Kathryn's demands because I felt guilty about leaving her father, about taking her away from her home by moving to California, and about getting remarried.

Kathryn is extremely smart. She knew just how to play me, and she was good at it. In the end, she wore me out.

After the divorce, she wanted to go live with her father. I told her that was absolutely not an option, and that she would stay with her brother and me in California.

When she turned fourteen, she came to me and said, "Mom, Dad is getting up there in years and I don't know how much longer he has to live."

"Is he ill?" I asked.

"No, Mom, and that's my point," she said. "He's getting on in years. I've spent time with you, and I know, understand, and love you so much. Now I need to go and get to know who my father is before he's gone. If he should die before I do that, I would never forgive myself, and you wouldn't forgive yourself for denying me my chance."

I gave her words careful consideration. I thought of the consequences of not letting her go, especially if something did happen to her father. Her arguments sounded logical enough to me.

Tony thought it was a colossal mistake. It wasn't that he didn't want Kathryn to be with her dad, but he felt she wouldn't have the same structure living with him as she did with us. Structure and boundaries: two very simple concepts that every parent has to understand.

Kathryn did go to spend the summer at her dad's, and she was more or less left to make decisions on her own. After that, she ended up shuffling back and forth between our home and her dad's. As a result, she had a difficult time adjusting to the rules that were imposed in either home. She chose to be where it was most comfortable for her at the time. It was during this chaotic time that Kathryn started to have difficulty coping with her life.

My relationship with Kathryn was tested beyond all limits. It sent me on an emotional roller coaster ride, leaving me feeling brittle, anxious, exhausted, and angry. Kathryn and I went through several stormy estrangements. We went for months at a time without speaking to each other. Talk about pain.

I used to pass judgment on people who said they weren't speaking to their children. I thought, *What in the world is wrong with these people? How could you not speak to your child? You must not be a very nice person if you can do that.*

It wasn't until I walked in their shoes that I realized not speaking to your child has nothing to do with not being a nice person or not loving your child. It's just that the situation gets so desperate that you actually need all the love you can muster in order to help them. You have to love them enough to let them go. You have to be strong to watch them make mistakes, not interfere, and let them suffer the consequences of their own actions.

I forced myself *not* to call Kathryn after our big blowout fights. If I called, we would start by having an innocent conversation, but somehow the volcano soon erupted and the conversation got ugly and became filled with verbal abuse. The words that came out of her mouth were something out of a science fiction movie. *Who acts like that? What in the world was this about?*

I couldn't understand why my daughter would speak to me like that. Knowing no better, I would end up yelling right back, which, of course, made things worse. It wasn't until much later that I realized I allowed her to react the way she did because I still felt guilty about the divorce.

After our fights, when she would finally call and I would hear her voice on the other end of the line, I would melt. Every single time. We would start up a fresh conversation as if nothing had happened. We never even mentioned the incident that sparked the estrangement in the first place. Most of the time, I couldn't even remember what the blowout was about.

I thought if I overlooked the blowouts, we could move on and pretend they never happened. I pretended they never happened in the past and would never happen in the future. Unfortunately, they did happen—again and again and again.

I can only compare this to dancing in a circle. We'd go around and around, having the same disagreements over and over. We must have found a hundred different ways to have the same argument. Nothing *ever* got resolved. It felt like we would put a bandage on our wounds, but then it would get ripped off and we'd bleed all over everything again. I needed to find a way to break out of this never-ending cycle. I didn't know what I was doing wrong. *Why was she so angry?*

I didn't know how to handle a child so out of control. I wasn't prepared for the chaos, lying, arguing, and disagreeing. We argued about her choice of clothes, the kind of friends she chose, curfews, tattoos, hair color, and grades—all the normal things that parents and teenagers disagree about. But unlike other teenagers, when Kathryn couldn't get her way, she became irrational and was prone to rage.

I had raised a child without setting boundaries for her. No one had said no and meant no, or even put restrictions on her behavior. As a result, when boundaries were put upon her, she didn't have the tools or the skills to cope.

—— ⋙ ——

Kathryn's episodes of rage left me feeling empty and desperate. I had control over *nothing,* not even my own emotions. I was so busy being angry with her that I took it out on everyone around me. There were other issues that we needed to deal with, but that is something that should remain private.

I needed help to aid my daughter. But I also needed to understand how to break this destructive behavior cycle that both of us were stuck in.

One Sunday, a friend asked if we would like to go to church with her to listen to a special guest speaker. "Who is it?" I asked.

"His name is Dr. Henry Cloud," she said. "I've heard him several times before, and I think he is just terrific. He's written many books, including a phenomenal one called *Boundaries.* I know you'll like him. Please come."

"Hmmm," I said. "Sure. Okay, I'll go."

So Tony, Alex, Ari, and I joined my friend at church. From the moment Dr. Cloud spoke his first word, I sat with my mouth wide open. Everything—and I mean *everything*—he was lecturing about was *exactly* what was happening in my life with Kathryn. He used a father-son scenario, but it could just as well have been Cristina-Kathryn.

I was flabbergasted. I thought he was speaking directly to me. My kids kept poking me and saying, "That's you and Kathryn, Mom! That's you and Kathryn." My side began hurting because they were poking me so much.

By the time Dr. Cloud finished, I knew I had to speak with this man. He knew and understood everything. He had answers to all of my questions about Kathryn! He understood the pain we were all in. He could help me fix the situation, I felt. I had to find him and talk to him. But after the service, he disappeared—vanished—and I was despondent.

As I searched around the church for Dr. Cloud, Tony came running up with a book in his hand. "Here, honey, I got you his book," he said. "Maybe it will help."

"I don't want the book!" I said in frustration. "I need to talk to him in person. Everything he said was so helpful and so true in my case. *I need to meet this guy!* I know he could help me."

But Dr. Cloud was gone and nobody could find him. So I took *Boundaries* and began reading it on the car ride home.

Back home, I called the church office to try to find Dr. Cloud. "He's on a lecture tour and unavailable for the next few months," I was told.

What happened next was unbelievable. Even now, it still amazes me. The day after I learned that Dr. Cloud would be on tour and unavailable for months, Tony called with some amazing news. He had just been asked to sit on the board of directors of the Los Angeles Mission, and he had gone there to meet the other directors for the first time that day.

"Hi, honey," he said. "Guess who's sitting right next to me?"

"Who?" I asked.

"Dr. Henry Cloud," he said.

"Shut up!" I screamed, and then began practically squealing. "Are you serious? I don't believe you. You're kidding me! Really? Oh my God, really?"

"You're not going to believe this, but he's on the board of directors here at the Mission!" Tony said, laughing.

"I need to speak to him," I said. "Please, honey, let's invite him over for dinner. I have to meet this man!"

Tony assured me he had it all covered. He had already told Dr. Cloud about what was going on with my life, and Dr. Cloud had agreed to meet with me. Tony put him on the phone. I acted like a groupie. (You would have thought I was meeting Elvis!) I spurted out ten years of turmoil, never stopping to catch my breath. I told him how moved I had been by his lecture. I told him how he had spoken to me on an emotional level and how desperate I was to learn more.

He agreed to meet with me. I was so nervous. He was my last hope, but I knew in my gut that he would be able to help me deal with my daughter.

I went to meet him at his home, where he introduced me to his beautiful wife, Tory, and their infant daughter. They were both so gracious, and I felt comfortable immediately. Dr. Cloud and I went into the back yard, where we sat under a tree and I spilled my guts out. He was extremely sympathetic, but the look on his face told me that he had heard this story a million times before. Oddly, this gave me a sense of relief; I realized that I wasn't the only mother who had problems like this with her children.

Dr. Cloud counseled me on my behavior, especially on how not to keep enabling my children. He gave me suggestions on how to access the tools I needed in order to be strong enough to set those boundaries he kept talking about. He handed me books and literature to read and help guide me. We also closed with a prayer for guidance, which I deeply appreciated. "Feel free to call on me any time," he said.

As he was walking me to my car, he told me that the Sunday sermon I heard was a departure for him. He confided that because he speaks at two separate services each Sunday, he usually speaks on the same subject for both services. But for some reason, he didn't use his lecture from that morning. Instead, he had felt compelled to speak about out-of-control teenagers and co-dependent relationships. Talk about the power of prayer!

I am eternally grateful to Dr. Cloud. His books have been an inspiration to me, and his guidance has helped me make sense out of teenage angst and chaos. I can tell you one thing I know for sure: Hang in there. It's true what they say: There is no greater love than the love of a parent for their child. So I hung in there, even though there were so many times I wanted to give up. But I didn't. Kathryn was worth fighting for, as all children are. Change didn't happen overnight, but it did happen, and we all learned from it.

The biggest lesson I learned was never to lose faith. The bonding you do with your children when they are small is never lost. You somehow find your way back to each other.

Kathryn is now twenty-six. As of this writing, she's just given birth to her second child, a beautiful baby girl, Acacia Rene, who joins her four-year-old brother, Kevin.

When Kathryn told me she was pregnant with Kevin, she wasn't as settled as she is today. I had prayed for so many years that she would straighten out and live a good and healthy life. Then I got the news that she was bringing a baby into the mess that I just knew she had made of her life. I was angry with God. I felt betrayed.

Is this the answer to my desperate cries? God sending an innocent child into Kathryn's calamitous life? I've now lived to eat those words and learned to ask forgiveness for my lack of faith. These two babies, these two beautiful souls, turned everyone's lives around, especially mine.

Kathryn is an outstanding mother and person. Motherhood

changed her dramatically. She turned herself around immediately. I'm proud of how hard she fought to straighten out her life.

Kathryn's two babies bring an added joy and new life into our family. I never thought I could love my grandkids as much as I love my own children, but I love them even more.

So we have come full circle, and I don't mean that circle dance. That's over. Kathryn and I can now disagree without everything boiling over every time in an ugly fight. We finally have a wonderful, loving, trusting relationship. I adore her and look forward to talking to her every day, and seeing her as much as possible.

She needs me. Not to make things better for her, but to offer a safe place to go for unconditional love and support. She still does things that make my hair stand on end. She loves motorcycles and fast cars. She has tattooed parts of her body that I didn't know you could, and her personality is larger than life. She is a complex, brilliant person.

Kathryn approaches life with far less caution than I do. My instinct is to protect, but I force myself to remember that I have to let go. It's a tough thing to do, but in the end, we are all better for it.

Ari and Alex after hiking up a big mountain.
I hope they can always keep their
great sense of humor and love of life.

Volleyball Mom

REMEMBER THIS ONE, MOM?" Alex exclaims, holding up a photograph. I laugh at the picture of her and Ari clowning around. Yet I also feel a pang of sadness. In the photo, the girls are on the verge of becoming teenagers. Once they did, their schedules were taken up with so many after-school activities that some days, I felt more like a chauffeur than their mom!

Still, I always felt proud of their achievements, and it was fun to cheer my daughter's on. One of Alex's many activities was being on a volleyball team. I remember watching in awe and excitement as I observed her and the other magnificent young women. They seemed so full of enthusiasm, energy, and anticipation.

It was almost surreal to watch Alex leap into the air to spike the ball over the net. Her ponytail swung like a pendulum from side to side as the rest of her teammates gave each other high-fives over a hard-won point. All of us parents were on our feet congratulating ourselves as if we had personally scored the point.

As I look at Alex now, I am suddenly struck by how much time has flown by. My mind races back to my own youth, when everything seemed possible. I remember that I wore the same expression that I observed in those girls' beautiful faces at the volleyball matches: a sense of determination mixed with a strong competitive streak. At their games, I could relive my girlhood; within their excitement was the possibility of greater things yet to come. They had goals, and nothing was going to stop them from achieving each and every one.

Then, as I look down at the box of photos, I suddenly feel sadness. It seems to come out of nowhere. I realize that my little girl has blossomed into a beautiful young woman. She and her teammates are just at the starting gate. I envy their situation. It seems like only yesterday that I was at the starting gate, poised to sprint forward with the rest of my life. That's when I remember Volleyball Mom.

I had met her at one of the volleyball games. I had been sitting there cheering Alex in the grandstands when she came over. She was the mother of one of Alex's teammates. I could immediately see from her face that something was deeply troubling her. I didn't know her all that well, only enough to say "Hello" at the games and in the carpool line at school. She wore a facial expression that I have noticed a lot of women wearing these days.

I've begun to recognize different facial expressions all too well. I've even made a list and categorized them. She had numbers four and five!

The list is called "Facial Expressions" from the book of *Ten Things I Wish Someone Had Warned Me About Before I Turned Thirty!*

1. I married my college sweetheart, and I don't know what has happened. *He's changed!*
2. I broke off with the love of my life, and I will never ever experience that kind of love again.

3. I lost my job. *Now what?*
4. My kids are almost grown. What am I going to do with the rest of my life?
5. I'm scared to go back out into the work force. What if I fail?
6. My husband just dumped me for a trophy wife after twenty years of marriage and three kids.
7. My husband died and left me with nothing except major debt.
8. Who's going to marry a menopausal woman with four kids and six grandchildren?
9. How do I change careers midstream?
10. How did I lose sight of the very essence of me?

I took her arm and we went to the side of the auditorium and sat down on some gym mats. As we started to sit—*before we could even hit the ground!*—she grabbed both of my arms and looked straight into my eyes. "I am so depressed and I don't know how to help myself!" she practically screamed, as if the phrase had been caught inside of her for decades.

I was stunned by her directness, and how she got right to the heart of the matter. I immediately felt empathy for her. Why she came to me, I don't know. Maybe she knew I had a list.

As she spoke, the volleyball game seemed to slip into slow motion and the crowd's thunderous screams and cheers diminished and became background noise. I didn't even have time to ask her why she was depressed. She offered up numbers four and five, just as I had suspected. "My kids are almost grown. What am I going to do with the rest of my life?" she blurted out. "I'm scared to go back to work. What if I fail?"

She then asked me in earnest, "How is it that you remain so busy and focused? You seem to have had many careers and career changes, and you keep right on going, seemingly without a problem?"

Yeah, right. Little did she know how I actually reacted to each major change in my life. To her, my life seemed to stay right on track. I decided to spare her the fantasy, and let it rip.

The words just came pouring out. "The one thing I know for sure is failure," I said. "But," I added, "I've never been one to lie down and give up when things go south. It may hurt and I may stay down for a bit, but I keep on getting up. For example, in my profession as talk show host, I worked on many different shows."

"Yes, I know," said Volleyball Mom, rattling off a couple of the cancelled series.

"Do you notice a trend?" I asked, interrupting her laundry list of daytime television programs. "The 'C' in my name should stand for 'cancel'. Every time one of my shows was canceled, I would flip out. But then I would eventually calm down and start to brainstorm other ways of generating income. It was always important for me to have my own paycheck. After all, I've been working since I was fourteen, and the idea of not earning my own way really tore at me. Maybe that's why I tried so many things. I experimented with a lot of different ideas, but I wasn't always successful."

The memories rushed back, one painful recollection after another.

I tried baking and selling cookies. "They were delicious, but I ended up eating most of the profits!" I told Volleyball Mom.

I took singing lessons and actually laid down some tracks on an album. "How I had the guts to try that one, I'll never know!" I said, adding that my tracks never got out of the studio.

I contacted one of the home shopping networks to see if they would be interested in Cristina Ferrare Personalized Pet Food Products. I don't even think my dogs were interested. "Must I go on with this list of embarrassing failures?" I asked Volleyball Mom.

She said, "Please continue," and so I did. I told her that every time one of my talk shows was canceled, I would be sent into a tailspin. "I would bitch and moan that my life was over, and *What was I going to do now?"* I admitted. "I would feel sorry for myself for a few days and make everyone around me miserable."

But, I added, it was usually during these "down" times that I would be able to tap into my creative side. "Everyone has one," I said. "And if you can learn to be still and listen to your inner voice, you can tap into an energy force that you don't even realize is there. I've learned that this is the first step to actually developing your creative side and getting it to grow."

"What do you mean?" she questioned.

"What do you like to do?" I asked. "No, wait, what do you have a *passion* for?"

She looked at me and said without hesitation, "I love writing and painting."

"So, why aren't you doing that?" I asked.

"I've only dabbled in it, and I don't even know if I'm any good at it," she said. "Besides, I don't have the time."

"Is it because of the kids?" I asked.

"Yes," she said, demurely.

Being my normally tactful self, I took her shoulders and gave her a strong shake and said, "Baloney! It's not that you don't have the time because of the kids. It's because you're scared. You're afraid of putting yourself back out there and maybe failing!

"Listen carefully," I said, "It's okay to be scared."

"It is?" she asked.

"Yes, it is," I reassured her. "I couldn't bring myself to take those first few steps each time either. I didn't believe in myself, I didn't believe in the gifts that I'd been given, that we all have been given. I would start sabotaging myself almost immediately. I'd haul out all of my 'What if?' excuses."

I recited the laundry list:

What if I'm not really good at what I love?

What if people laugh at me and think I'm being foolish?

What if I can't take this dream and move to the next level?

What if I can't make a career out of this?

What if I can't generate any income?

What if I can't stand any more rejection?

"Stop the 'What ifs!'" I said. "Stop making excuses, and just do it!"

I told her the story of how I began to write. It was during one of my down times, when I was trying to figure out what to do next. I knew the direction I wanted to take was toward what I loved. So my initial thought was, *Okay, find your passion.* I believe passion is the driving force in all of us.

For as long as I can remember, my passion has been food and cooking. I decided to parlay that passion by writing down family recipes and the memories they evoked when I was growing up. I prepared the recipes and photographed the food myself. I put the pictures and recipes in a little book and added personal anecdotes here and there. After it was completed, I gave it to my mom to read.

She loved it. (What can I say—she's my mom.)

I then hesitatingly gave it to my husband Tony to read. I say "hesitatingly" because he is brutally honest and I really did want him to love it. *He did!* But I couldn't believe him. I thought he was being too nice. Why didn't I believe him? I wanted his approval, but when I got it, I turned and questioned his sincerity. For some reason, I'd later realize, I was sabotaging my own work.

My thoughts were mutinous: *What's wrong with me? Why can't I accept the fact that maybe it is good? After all, didn't I want it to be good?*

I needed to have faith in my gift and believe in myself.

I thought my book was good until everyone started telling me it *was* good. *Now what? Oh, I see: Now that people have told me it's good, I actually have to go out there and try to get it published.* That's it.

"I was afraid of failure," I told Volleyball Mom. "If the book was no good, I could just put it away and forget about going any further with it. Play it safe. Not put myself on the line. I'd think, *I'm not going to a publisher because it's really not that good. Or is it?*"

Deep down inside, I knew I had created a good cookbook. But I was scared that if I sent it to a publisher and it was turned down, I would have to deal with rejection again. The whole reason why I started the book in the first place was to get over my last rejection. So the last thing I wanted to do was to face yet another rejection.

With Tony prodding me to move forward, I hesitatingly began the process. I didn't even know what "the process" was. I just kind of threw it out there. I called and networked with everyone I knew. My girlfriend Maria suggested that I meet with her literary agent who was coming into town from Dallas. Maria thought it would be a great fit. *Sure, why not; I'll talk to a literary agent.*

I met with Jan Miller. I soon discovered she wasn't any old book agent. I found out she was a big-time literary agent with a gigantic roster of big-time, best-selling authors. I was scared to death.

We met over breakfast, and I fell in love with her immediately! We connected with our mutual enthusiasm for food and family. We just talked and talked and talked. She loved the idea of my family cookbook, and when I sent her the actual book, she loved it, too. "I'll have no problem getting this published," she said.

With those words resonating in my ears, I then tried to get out of doing it.

I started to sabotage myself almost immediately. I told Jan I couldn't possibly get away to do a book tour because I couldn't be away from the kids that long. She told me not to worry. She had spoken with Tony, and he was prepared to cover for me at home.

Next I told her that the book contained old family recipes handed down from generation to generation, and if my grandmother knew I was sharing them outside the family, it would kill her. I didn't bother to tell Jan that Grandmother had been dead for two years.

Tony pointed out to me that I needed to stop this destructive behavior and stop being afraid to move onto the next level. So, basically, I just let myself be pushed along while I kept digging in my heels. There was a lot of editing and double-checking and triple-checking that went into it because it was a cookbook and every measurement had to be precise. We also had to have the recipes tested. I went along with the process.

I finished the book and turned it in. It had taken me more than a year to complete, but I did it and that's the important thing. It was published and I went on the book tour. The kids did fine. I had a great time. Just like that, I launched my mini-career as an author.

I went on to write my second book, *Okay, So I Don't Have a Headache.* It was about women who lose their sex drive and why it happens. I had lost mine and needed to fix it. Again, during one of my down times, I started doing research on health and nutrition specifically for women and just started writing. Talk about finding your passion—I needed to get my mojo in working order again. I loved working on the book. It was received very well: So well, in fact, that I was asked to go on Oprah Winfrey's show to talk about it. It even made *The New York Times* bestseller list! It started conversations around the country that encouraged people to find solutions to this very real problem. I think it helped a lot of women.

Meanwhile, I had to help myself. The whole book experience had been a key. It had unlocked a hidden passion deep within me. I discovered I really loved to write. I developed an exhilaration that I never expected. I learned that I had skills I never knew I possessed. I had the ability to communicate to people through the written word.

Will I be able to make a living from books? Maybe yes, maybe no; it doesn't matter right now. What matters is that writing makes me happy. I do it for the pleasure and satisfaction that it gives me. That satisfaction is especially great when someone comes up to me to tell me how much she enjoys the cookbook or how much my *Okay* book has helped her.

Even though my books were doing well, there was something else that was bubbling up inside of me. Once again, I decided to dig deep and call up my personal reserves. *What else was I passionate about?* I figured that I was bound to hit on something sooner or later that would be just what I've been searching for. I kept pursuing the "road less traveled," to quote a favorite inspirational poem by Robert Frost.

Completely unexpectedly, I unlocked an inner passion during another one of my down times. I had dabbled in painting before, but hadn't thought much about it for years. Then one day I took my kids to one of those paint-your-own-ceramics stores. I thought it would be just a fun family activity, but as we all sat around the table and painted our bowls, I totally lost myself in the process.

The texture of the paints, their vivid colors, and the feel of the brush on the grainy surface of the ceramic was an immediate turn-on. *What's that all about?* Everything about the experience made me realize that I wanted to do more of it.

After dropping the kids off at school, I would head down to the ceramic paint store and spend all the time I could there. It opened up a whole new world of feelings, expressions, and creativity that somehow brought out a sense of accomplishment and, for lack of a better word, peace.

I photographed my pieces and assembled the photographs in a book. I talked to everyone and eventually learned about starting a business manufacturing and selling ceramics. Because this was all new to me, I relied on networking, just as I had done when I learned how to get my cookbook published.

There is a wealth of information on the Internet on how to start your own business. There's information on how to secure a small business loan to help set up your business and different manufacturing and distributing companies to help with merchandising. The more I researched, the more I learned that it's not all that hard to do.

Who would have guessed that I would be getting into ceramics? My product development is simple. I go into stores that sell the types of items I create, and I talk to the store owner. I ask questions about what they look for when they purchase new items, and what sorts of things sell best. You'd be surprised how much information you can gather if you just go out and talk to people. If you have a passion for what you're doing, all this information gathering is actually fun.

Modeling, acting, hosting talk shows, writing, painting—I realize that these experiences are a process, a journey if you will, of one thing leading to another. Who knows what I'll end up doing next? I just throw it out there, see what happens, and grasp the opportunities when they stare me in the face.

—— ⚘ ——

"One thing we know for sure, nothing stays the same," I told Volleyball Mom. "Eventually, the road will curve and you will be faced with something new and different. It's what you do with the change and how you handle it that will define who you are as a person."

After I finished my long story, pouring out my soul to this woman who seemed to so desperately need my help, we were both drawn back into the moment at hand by thunderous screams and stomping of feet. The volleyball game was over. We had been so caught up in our conversation that we didn't even know the final score or the winning team. But a quick look at Alex's face told me that it wasn't us.

I gave Volleyball Mom a hug. "If you need to talk more, call me," I said, and I gave her my telephone number.

On the way to the car, I carried Alex's backpack, which always weighed a ton. I felt bad that they lost the game. I automatically went into rescue mode to try to make her feel better by doing everything for her. Once we were in the car, I took her hand, squeezed it, and told her how sorry I was that they lost.

"That's okay, Mom," she said with authority. "You can't always win. I'm disappointed, but I'll deal with it. There's always another game. Besides, didn't you always tell us, 'Losing is soup for the soul? It's how you deal with defeat that helps define you as a person?' I'll be fine!" Then, she squeezed back.

I looked heavenward and said to myself, "Thank you, God. She gets it."

Then, I thought, *She's right. Defeat* does *help define you as a person.*

It took me a while to really understand this. First, I had to go through several failures, but eventually I came out on the other side, stronger for the journey.

—— ⚘ ——

Driving Alex home, I began to pour out my heart. The experience with Volleyball Mom had touched something deep within me, and I wanted to pass it on immediately.

Just like Volleyball Mom needed me, I told Alex, I need my girl-friends. At times, I find myself needing to look beyond my immediate family for support. I need to have reinforcements. I need my girl-friends, and thank God, I have a few great ones. I love women. I love who we are. I totally embrace our sexuality and our power. I'm sorry it took me so long to realize how to wield that power. I feel confident we are able to do anything we want and accomplish anything we desire.

I love being feminine and all the fun stuff that goes with it—the hair, clothes, purses, perfumes, stockings, and high heels. I celebrate the fact that we are different from men and that they don't understand us at times. I love that we sometimes play games to further confuse them (and, *no,* guys, I'm not going to reveal any of them here).

By nature, we women are nurturing and fiercely protective of our families and friends. For those of us who choose to have children, the intensity of our love knows no bounds. There are no sacrifices too difficult to endure when it comes to our loved ones.

I love the qualities that allow us to be strong, protective, soft, loving, vulnerable, and intense. I love that we cry, show emotion, and wear make-up. I love having girlfriends. We share our most intimate details with one another without embarrassment.

My girlfriends and I talk about everything, though we mostly talk about our children and how our lives were changed after we had them. When children enter the picture, *everything* changes. Your life is forever altered. You put your goals and your desires aside; your priorities become different. You are so involved in your kids' lives that there's little time to think about yourself.

Even if you're a working mom with a career that you love, you make concessions and choices that fit your family's needs and not yours.

You abandon the fairy tale for the reality.

—— ⚚ ——

A good example of shifting priorities happened to me when my son Zach was two. I had just returned home to L.A. from New York, where I had been for a week on a modeling assignment. I was happy to see "Z" and glad to be home with my family, for what I hoped would be a long time.

Then the phone rang. It was my agent, and she was breathless.

"I can't wait to tell you some incredible news!" she said.

I had been booked by *Vogue* magazine for three weeks in Europe to appear in the fall fashion collection.

I think she assumed I was too shocked to answer. Instead of snapping up the opportunity, I took a pass. I told my agent that I appreciated the opportunity, but I couldn't be away from my baby for three weeks.

"Cristina, you're out of your mind," she said. "Do you know what you're doing? Girls kill for an opportunity like this!"

"I know," I said. "But Zach is too little, and I just don't want to be away from him again. I just got home."

Don't think I didn't remember every word of this many years later when Zach was a teenager and told me he hated my guts because I wouldn't let him dye his hair green.

Somewhere between losing your sanity during your children's teenage years and getting them off to college or a job, you begin to pick up the little pieces of yourself again.

That's when another reality hits. For some marriages, this time is part of the "worse" aspect of the marriage vow, but it can be an opportunity for much more of the "better." As the need to mother our children diminishes, reality takes a big bite out of our hearts. You are not needed or depended upon as much. The kids don't need you to dress or feed them. They don't even need you to take them to school; they drive themselves. No more schlepping them to Little League, soccer practice, basketball, ice-skating lessons, ballet, gymnastics, art classes, music lessons, play rehearsals, Spanish lessons, karate, or tutoring sessions. They can get there themselves. Your taxiing days are over.

As my kids gained their independence, I needed a little help from my friends. The question we all asked ourselves was this: "What in the world am I going to do with all this free time?"

We realized that this was a time for reflection. This was the time to look to the very essence of who we really were and to regain our own independence. Here are some of the questions that I had to ask myself. At some point, you'll probably have to ask the very same questions, too:

Why was I so good at my chosen profession (the one you may have abandoned to become a wife and mother) in the first place?

What qualities made my mate fall in love with me to begin with?

Why do my friends adore me?

Why did I give everything I had to raising the kids, being a supportive spouse, and being a caring, nonjudgmental friend?

Don't lose yourself in denial, and never buy into the always bogus feeling that you don't have anything to offer anymore. Talk with other women for help on tapping into ideas that you want to make happen. And, when possible, use your own experiences to mentor other women.

Don't be afraid to be afraid.

The best thing we've got going for us as women is our ability to share our feelings and communicate what we want. Use it. Share it with a friend. You'll be amazed at the strength that will grow from there.

Women accomplish so many things with our natural ability to multitask. With our network of women friends, the possibilities are endless. Now I know why they named that women's network "Oxygen." It's because we suck it right out of the room with our energy!

I had been driving on autopilot while I poured my heart out to Alex. When I reached the "Oxygen" comment, she looked at me dumbfounded and said, "Gee Mom, all this because I lost a volleyball game? Were you always like this? Sometimes I think you're psycho! Yeah, you're a psycho, but interesting."

We remained silent for the rest of the ride home. I kept looking over at her and thinking how much I loved her and how proud I was of the young woman she has become.

——— ✿ ———

I'm thrilled to say that Volleyball Mom now owns a trendy store in Santa Monica where she sells her own works of art along with those of other artists. I'm proud of her, just as I'm proud of Alex.

I hope that Alex can learn from my mistakes so she doesn't have to repeat them. But the reality is, even if she avoids *my* mistakes, she'll make plenty of her own. The other reality is that confronting her mistakes will make her stronger to face whatever life throws her way.

Starting a jewelry business with my mother
unleashed a hidden passion I never knew I had.
What's next? Only time will tell!

Starting Over

HECK THIS ONE OUT, MOM," Arianna says, as she hands me a recent photo from one of the last stacks we haven't yet tackled.

In the photo, I'm wearing a necklace and matching earrings from my jewelry line.

How did I get into the jewelry-making business?

It happened by accident, as most opportunities do.

I was doing a daily talk show called *Men Are from Mars, Women Are from Venus.* I was busy shooting two shows a day and hardly had time for anything other than my family. I enjoyed doing the show, and it helped me get past being rejected for the co-hosting job with Regis Philbin. But true to form, my new show got canceled.

It was then that I realized I needed to rethink this whole talk show thing. I had to move on. I was nervous, though, and wondered what in the world I was going to do now.

One afternoon my mother came to see me, holding a bunch of beaded necklaces. "What are those?" I asked.

"Necklaces I made for the kids," she said. "They liked them so much they asked if I would make some they could give to their friends as Christmas gifts."

They were so adorable that I came up with a suggestion. "You know, Mom, these are so wonderful that I bet you could make extra cash by selling them," I said.

"Who's going to buy them?" she asked. "Besides, I don't know the first thing about selling outside of a store." My mother has an extensive background in retail sales; she used to be one of the managers and designers for Italian fashion giant Gucci.

"Well, why don't you show me how to help you make them, and I'll invite friends over for a tea and we can sell them," I said. "It's perfect because everyone will be looking for Christmas and Hanukkah gifts. You can use whatever money we make to take a trip to Italy and visit the relatives!"

The next day, Mom took me downtown to The Jewelry Mart, a tiny bead store where we had to pick up a phone and call an attendant to "buzz" us in. People were packed like sardines into that little store. We needed a ticket just to purchase our items.

"Serving number fifty-one!" the clerk yelled. We were number seventy-two. For some reason, I wasn't discouraged. I had my mom hold our place in line while I went to get us sandwiches and cappuccinos. As we ate our lunch, the place thinned out a bit. I took a look around me and saw floor-to-ceiling beads, pearls, and crystals in every color imaginable. It looked like something out of Aladdin's Treasure Chest.

I thought I had finally fallen into one of my childhood fairy tales. There were sparkles everywhere, and it was all mine for the taking— after I paid for it, of course.

"What is this place?" I finally asked Mom.

She explained that we were in the heart of the jewelry district, and this was where many jewelers would go to buy their wares, which, she said, were called "findings." I stood there with my mouth open in amazement. After I closed it, I bought enough findings to choke a horse.

It was one of those defining moments. It didn't seem like such a big deal at the time, but it turned out to be perhaps one of the biggest deals in my entire life.

After we made our purchases, we returned to my house and got down to the business of beading. I rounded up Alex and Ari and even brought my dad in to help. Tony wasn't even remotely interested in beading. After dinner, we all sat around the kitchen table and my mother showed us how to bead the necklaces onto "memory wire," which is wire that wraps around your neck to form a necklace without the need for a clasp.

After a while, we started to compete to see who could come up with the most creative piece. My dad, of all people, won by using the most unusual color combinations. By the end of the evening, we had made more than three hundred pieces. Both the kitchen and the dining room tables were covered with necklaces.

"Good Lord," I said when I realized what we had done. "How in the world am I going to sell all of these necklaces? I don't even *know* three hundred people. Tony's going to kill me!"

It was like an *I Love Lucy* episode. We tried to find places to hide all of the necklaces before Tony found out what we had done. We stuffed them behind the sofa and under the bed. Then I began going through our Rolodex to send out invitations to our necklace-selling holiday party.

We held the tea party in the afternoon. Lots of my friends showed up, and they brought their friends. Not only did they all love the necklaces, they bought them in bulk. Because the necklaces cost only

$20 to $35 apiece, they bought gifts for everyone on their holiday lists. At the end of the day, we were completely sold out.

I counted the receipts over and over again. I couldn't believe we actually made a profit! When I finished counting for the last time, I handed the money over to my mom and wished her a happy trip to Europe. She smiled and asked me if I would like to come along. "My treat," she said.

I told her I wanted to buy more beads to make more necklaces. I was completely obsessed with what I saw in that tiny bead store. All I could think about was making jewelry.

My mother not only agreed, but she said she wanted me to reinvest all of our profits. "We can start a small jewelry company together, Cristina," she said. "You can design, and I'll keep the books." We shook hands, and we were in business.

We headed back downtown and waited in line again. I loved everything I saw. I probably purchased more than we needed, but I was obsessed! I wanted to turn every bead, crystal, and pearl into necklaces, earrings, and bracelets. I came up with an eclectic collection that lacked any sense of continuity, which, I later learned, is an essential element when you present a jewelry collection to buyers. But at the time, I didn't care about continuity. The jewelry was pretty and that's all that mattered.

This time around, Mom and I hired professional beaders to string and wire the jewelry. We also decided to design for women instead of kids, which increased the price tags.

A few weeks later, I sent out invitations to another tea party. Once again, lots of people showed up. My girlfriends came through for me and were extremely supportive and helpful in giving me advice and encouragement. One of my girlfriends, Nadine, spent the whole day with me, greeting other friends and helping me sell a lot of necklaces. My other friend Annie did the same, and brought women who did some serious buying.

Seeing people respond so positively to my jewelry gave me incentive. I can't really explain it; all I knew was that I wanted to make jewelry and sell it. I wanted to start a business.

I knew absolutely nothing about the jewelry trade or major retail. Setting up an office to handle day-to-day business and dealing with overhead were foreign to me. To me, overhead was the trouble I got into every month when I had to face my charge accounts. I was in *wa-a-a-a-y* over my head.

Ironically, my ignorance and lack of experience actually helped me open the first major door. I didn't understand the protocol about whom I was supposed to call. I just picked up the phone and called John Martins, the general manager of the Beverly Hills Neiman Marcus store.

"I'd like to meet with you to show you my new line of jewelry," I said. "Would you be kind enough to let me come by at your convenience?"

I'm not totally naïve! I know that Mr. Martins only agreed to meet with me out of politeness. I'll admit that hosting a talk show helps, but once I got in the door, I had to deliver. It turns out that Mr. Martins liked what he saw and called in Michele Girrade, the manager of the designer jewelry department, to take a look at my pieces as well.

I asked them if they would agree to let me have a trunk show in their store. They agreed.

The show was a success, and everyone was happy. I asked if they would consider putting some of my pieces in their Neiman Marcus store on consignment, just to see how they would do. Again they agreed, and, again, the pieces sold.

My next move was to go to Neiman Marcus headquarters in Dallas. I wanted to meet with the buying office to see if they would purchase my collection. This experience turned out to be a lesson in humility and patience.

I confidently ventured into the massive downtown Dallas flag-
ship store, rolling my little suitcase filled with what I thought was
a fabulous collection. I sat with the other vendors who were waiting
to show their wares, until I was finally escorted into a tiny confer-
ence room. I carefully unrolled my jewelry rolls and waited another
forty-five minutes. At last, a lovely girl with flaming red hair in a
pageboy walked in. I was surprised to see that she looked barely
sixteen.

She proceeded to tell me what was wrong with my collection. "Go
home, fix it, do another trunk show in Beverly Hills, and see how you
do," she said. "If all goes well, the managers will purchase the collection for the Beverly Hills store."

She rose and walked to the door. "Thank you, and good luck," she
said.

Okay, I can do this. I can take direction from someone who is
younger than some of my children.

I had begun what would be a crash course in retail. I had to learn
everything from the ground up. Like everything else in life, it was a
process.

I totally embraced this whole new world. I've never worked so
hard at anything in my entire life. I wanted to succeed at my new career more than anything I'd ever done. So I immersed myself in jewelry and learned everything I could about design, manufacturing,
marketing, and client relations.

We started with one store, and with the support of Michele
Girrade, the designer jewelry manager at Neiman Marcus in Beverly
Hills, we were quickly one of their best-selling vendors. That was
only four years ago. Our jewelry is now in fifteen Neiman Marcus
stores, and we have expanded into Saks Fifth Avenue and Geary's of
Beverly Hills.

I realize this all sounds like a big success story, and it is. However, I've learned that success has several sides with "caution" written all over them. There are "up" sides and "down" sides, and you need to be prepared to deal with all of them.

Coming up with three distinct collections each year is a huge responsibility. Each store needs thirty-five pieces. Multiply that by thirty to forty stores, with the possibility of many more, and it's essential that you're on top of everything. You must keep abreast of fashion trends, the buying habits of the public, your cash flow, the buying offices, and the shipping and handling of all your goods. All of this I could not do without Susan Cohn and Susana Kobritz. Susan runs the day-to-day operations and oversees all the shipping, ticketing, handling, and computer inventory. She is the hub of the office. Susana has the difficult task of keeping me in order; she's the cog in the wheel of the office operations. My mother keeps the books. I have created a triangle and feel protected. I firmly believe that the smartest thing you can do for yourself is surround yourself with people who are better than you. No man (or woman) is an island. I'm not ashamed to admit that I am not the end-all and be-all. This is definitely a team effort.

I really wanted my line to expand to more retail outlets, but I didn't have a clue as to how to accomplish that. So, I asked my husband, Tony, if he would get involved and help me grow the company.

"Honey, I need your help," I said in my best businesswoman voice. "I'm stuck. I need you to take over this company and help me bring it to the next level. This is your area of expertise. I've seen you do it with other companies. How about helping me with mine?"

"You mean *ours*," he corrected.

"Yeah, well, whatever," I said. "What do you say?"

"No," he said.

"No?" I repeated, startled. "What do you mean, 'No!' Are you serious?"

"I'm absolutely serious," he said firmly. "We both know that you're not going to take advice from me. You'll argue with me when you disagree, just like you do about everything at home. You'll continue arguing with me until you wear me out! No thank you, Cristina. You wear me out enough at home. I don't need to have it at the office."

"Well, it's certainly nice to know your true feelings," I said in a huff. But I didn't storm out. Not until I got what I wanted. "Come on, Tony, I really need your help here. Why should I pay some outside person when I've got the best right here in you? I'll tell you what: If you don't tell me how to design, I won't tell you how to run the business. I promise. Agreed?"

He thought about it a long time. Then, he finally looked up and shook his head. A little smile crossed his face, and I knew I had him.

"Okay," he said at last. "Agreed." We sealed it with a kiss.

It took Tony just six months to take my business to the next step, and then some. He brought a team of people over from a company called Creative Brands Group, headed by Ken Raasch, the moving force behind the "Thomas Kinkade" brand. Thomas Kinkade is considered to be America's best-selling living artist today.

Through them, I had found something that was everything I could have ever hoped for. Tony and Creative Brands came up with an idea that would incorporate all of the things I had managed to accomplish over the years. These included painting on ceramics, experimenting with different recipes, writing, decorating, and a host of other things I tried so I could keep my mind off of me during my "down times." They helped form and create a "brand," which would include a line of furniture, ceramics, books, and accessories.

This opportunity opened another door, another new world of possibilities. It allowed me to move on to the next phase in my life, my heart open to new adventures and new challenges. I was ready for the good as well as the not-so-good, because I knew that life never gives you one without the other. I understood that I would have happy days and bad days—sometimes in the same twenty-four hours.

So many people are still looking for the secret to living out their dreams. They want to live in the rarified world of ad-land, where everything is picture perfect. But I've learned that accepting life for what it is, and not for what we think it should be, is the most liberating experience on earth.

To be able to appreciate the moment and the power of the present is incredibly empowering. I had always been searching for perfection, trying to fool myself into believing that until I found it, I would never find true peace. I had set myself up for a never-ending cycle of disappointment. I was able to break free of it only when I finally was able to accept each experience for what it was at that particular moment in time. No more focusing on the "what ifs" and "if onlys." I had to learn that everything is subject to change, and that change is the only constant.

I finally realized that I could stop fighting. Fighting to always be the biggest and the best. Fighting to be successful at every single thing I tried. Fighting to have the perfect marriage and the perfect, most well-adjusted kids. Fighting to be loved by everyone I ever met. And, perhaps most importantly, fighting to be really thin in order to feel good about myself.

——— ⚹ ———

Learning to love my body and not worry about the number on the scale has been an ongoing process. But at least I've realized that it isn't necessary for me to be a size six in order for people to accept me. I finally accept myself as I am, and that's good enough. It took me a lifetime to arrive at this point, and now my only regret is that I didn't get help with this problem earlier in my life. I see now that I used eating as a cover-up for so many things. There was the Heavy Cristina and the Thin Cristina. I could hide in the Heavy Cristina, wrapping her up in layers of fat and clothes so I didn't have to face the harsh realities in my life. The Thin Cristina attracted people who I didn't want to allow too close because I feared that if they really knew me, I wouldn't be good enough or smart enough for them. So I kept her covered up.

Weight is something I still battle every day. It's an issue that sometimes requires professional help, and I've gotten some. Yes, I've learned to live with it. Yes, it is something that I'll most likely have to deal with for the rest of my life. That's the reality of it. Weight issues are based on emotion, and because dealing with stress, frustrations, and other emotions is a part of daily life, so is dealing with weight issues.

I feel so much for people who are looking for ways to lose all those pounds for the hundredth time. I want to tell them what I've learned as I endlessly yo-yo'd up and down the scale: *You're never going to find the answer in some crazy diet or pill. Stop eating the foods that make you fat, period. You know what they are. That's what it takes.*

I'm not saying it's okay to be significantly overweight. I think that anyone who does say that is doing a huge disservice to themselves. It is not healthy to carry around extra fat, period. It can lead to heart attacks, strokes, diabetes, and endless other health problems. When we talk about weight, the message should be about one thing: health.

Eating habits—not food—are the culprit in weight gain. Nothing is fattening if your daily intake of food is kept in balance with your metabolism and the calories you expend. But if you are eating for other reasons, if you're eating to sabotage yourself, as I was, you need to take a hard look at yourself.

I know that it's tough to stop overeating. There is no easy solution. I wish I could promise you that if you follow a certain diet and stick with it for the rest of your life, you'll be thin. But the truth is that there is no magic answer. You need to follow your head. I've learned that it is the head that usually needs fixing first. Then you can make sensible choices. Most people know what will make them stay heavy. Only you can control what goes into your mouth. Only you can control your life.

After a long, hard struggle, I've finally taken control of my life. Here's what I learned:

- Trust in God and His infinite wisdom. Even in my darkest hours, when I was scared and thought I was alone, I wasn't.
- It's okay to be scared.
- You have to acknowledge the hurt before it will stop.
- Setbacks are temporary and sometimes necessary.
- Don't be afraid to acknowledge your "gift." We all have one, often several. It is a God-given talent. Find it, nurture it,

and—once you own it—don't be afraid to turn it to your best advantage.

- Keep moving forward, no matter what happens.
- Be cautious, but keep moving.
- Finding your passion is the key to everything life has to offer.
- Let yourself be still, really still, and then listen to that voice that speaks to you from within.
- Recognize when you begin to sabotage yourself.
- You can't find happiness in chocolate.
- You're the only one who is going to feel sorry for you.
- Recognize the danger of getting too comfortable with the feeling of feeling bad.
- Keep yourself open to an opportunity even when you don't think it's the right move.
- Success should come with a caution label.
- Sometimes the answer is as close as your heart.
- Failure: it's a good thing.
- Get some help and let go of the past.
- When you're faced with an experience that you don't understand, accept it for what it is at that particular moment in time. Things are invariably going to change and you will need to move on.
- Forgive yourself.
- Forgive others. It will set you free!

Finally, I've learned that life is real, not a fairy tale. There is no Prince Charming who can rescue you from yourself. You will feel better about yourself and everyone else in your life when you personally take on that responsibility.

"Fairy tales are for children's books," I tell my girls as we fill the last box before we are officially ready to move into a brand-new home from the only house they've ever known. "Remember, there is no happily ever after, but the possibilities in life are endless! Let's go find some new ones!"

Christmas 2003: Ari, me, Alex, and Tony. Time marches on,
but with each other, we can face anything!

Fairy Tales
with a Twist

WHEN I WAS LITTLE, I couldn't wait for Sunday nights, when *The Wonderful World of Disney* would come on television. My sisters and I would sit there with our eyes, hearts, and minds wide open, awaiting the journey that these fairy tales would take us on.

I remember sitting on the floor so we could get as close to the TV as possible. We would inch up until our noses practically touched the screen, only to hear Dad exclaim, "You're going to ruin your eyes if you sit too close!" We would scoot back a few inches, eagerly awaiting the moment when Tinker Bell, with her tiny golden bun on top of her head, touched down from the heavens. We giggled with delight as she sprayed glitter all over the screen with her magic wand and transformed the TV screen into a wonderland of magic and imagination.

When the animated movies *Snow White and the Seven Dwarfs*, *Cinderella*, and *Sleeping Beauty* came out, I believed that everyone had a fairy godmother—sometimes three of them—flitting around with a jolly face and a congenial name like Merriweather!

All it took to make your life perfect was one wave of a magic wand. A handsome prince with a voice from heaven and dancing feet like Fred Astaire would come along to whisk you up onto his sturdy white horse. We'd live happily ever after.

I bought it all, big-time. I didn't have a wicked anything in my life. There was nothing to stand in my way. I would get lost in my imagination and think of what my life was going to be like when I grew up, met my prince, and lived my perfect life on Storybook Lane.

When Alex and Arianna were little, I read to them the same fairy tales I had loved as a child. As they listened to me read and followed along with the colorful pictures, I could see them being swept away by the story, just as I had been so many years before.

It was then that I decided I would put a different spin on the stories. After all, it was the 1990s, and I had certainly gained a lot of wisdom on my way to Oz.

I wanted to know what would happen if I told my girls the more probable "reality" version of the fairy tales. I wondered what would have happened in my own life if I had heard real-life renditions of fairy tales, which I began calling "Fairy Tales with a Twist," instead of the sugarcoated fantasy version that could never happen in a million years? Would it have made me less idealistic, less willing to believe in fantasy? I thought I owed my girls a chance at the real thing.

I wanted my daughters to keep in mind that at the end of the "Yellow Brick Road" was an ordinary man. I wanted them to remember that it's not about reaching for what you think will give you the answer, it is about the journey itself. Dorothy found her happiness when she looked to her heart and realized that she had the power all along to make the difference in her own life. Turning to some of my favorite childhood stories, I used Cinderella, Snow White, and

Sleeping Beauty to drive home my point: Reality fractures the fairy tale every time.

Cinderella, as everyone knows, had a kind heart and great compassion for the less fortunate. After the prince finally found her and the shoe fit, he wanted to marry her. Even though she loved him, she decided to wait to get married until she finished her college education. "She wanted to be a lawyer," I told my girls.

After she earned her law degree, she used her expertise to help children who came from abusive homes much like hers. It became important to her to help children everywhere to have a better life and to prosecute the abusive. Cinderella did end up marrying the prince, and her chosen profession made her happy and fulfilled.

After the birth of their first baby, she was still able to practice law and help others while she kept busy as a wife and mother. It wasn't always easy to juggle so many responsibilities, and she struggled with finding time for both her clients and her family. She often would put her own needs aside and sometimes would feel overwhelmed as she tried to keep the very essence of who she was as a person.

She had great comfort in knowing that if anything went wrong and she needed help, she could rely on her family for support. And if anything happened to her husband, she would be able to continue to provide for her family. She'll always have that law degree. That gave her a great sense of security and power in her own right.

Then there was Snow White. We all know how maternal she was just by the way she took care of the seven dwarfs. After the prince woke her with a kiss, he "had her at hello," as they say in the movies. Ms. White fell madly in love with Mr. Prince and wanted to marry him right away.

She realized, however, that she needed to slow down and get to know him first before taking such a serious step. She remembered a promise she had made to her father many years before he died: to finish high school and get her college degree.

Her father understood how much she loved the arts. Snow loved to sing and write music, and he had encouraged her to follow her heart. She kept her promise to her father and earned a bachelor's degree in music and a master's in art history.

Snow loved to cook and became an accomplished chef. Friends from all over the forest would hop, skip, fly, and jump from miles around to sample the delicious delicacies from her kitchen. Cooking, singing, and writing music filled her soul and made her happy. She felt satisfied with her personal goals and was ready to settle down and start a family. She was ready to make her commitment to her husband-to-be.

It was time to plan the wedding. She set the forest tables on the stumps of trees, then picked the copious wildflowers and arranged them in beautiful bouquets. She planned and cooked the dinner herself. After all, she was used to cooking for seven dwarfs.

She wrote a beautiful poem to her husband on their wedding day and composed a song that touched his heart deeply. She sang it to him in her angelic voice. Her father would have been proud. There wasn't a dry eye in the house.

Snow White and her prince decided to have children immediately. She made the choice to be a stay-at-home mom. They had three children but realized they had room in their hearts for many more, so they completed their family by adopting two more children. Snow immersed herself in her new role as mother. Their home was filled with an abundance of love. The house was always filled with music and wonderful aromas wafting from the kitchen.

The couple passed on to their children a sense of stability. They taught the youngsters to appreciate life and depend on one another, both in good times and bad. Life in the forest wasn't all that easy. Fighting to prevent forest fires and strip mining became a cause for Snow. Through her actions, she taught her kids that they needed to be strong in their conviction to help make a difference in the world.

Snow White was happiest when her house was full, especially when her seven little friends from down the way would visit her after a long day in the mines. Snow had a lot of irons in the fire. She could do *anything*. She was smart. She was accomplished. She was loved. She was a woman!

Finally, we arrived at the story of Sleeping Beauty. (By the way, what's with all these women who sleep all the time? Why do they need a prince to kiss them to make everything all right? And why is the guy always a prince? Why can't he be a shoe salesman?)

Thank goodness this prince was the type of person who refused to let anyone take advantage of him. And he would never assume he could kiss a sleeping woman without her permission. Sometimes, a simple touch of a hand can make you melt.

Sleeping Beauty's prince simply knelt down beside her and held her hand. She opened her eyes, awakened by love. The moment their eyes met, she felt as if she had known him all of her life.

After she brushed her teeth, they talked and talked and talked.

They had so much in common! Both were born to very wealthy families. They loved to talk about places they would go. They both had gypsy souls and loved to travel.

Although her back was killing her from lying in one position for so long, Beauty didn't want their first encounter to ever end. Deep down in her heart, she knew one day they would marry.

Before Aurora pricked Beauty's finger, sending her to sleep, Beauty had completed courses in investment banking. Because the prince owned all of the banks in his kingdom, Sleeping Beauty was a perfect mate for him.

The couple was painfully aware of how fortunate they were to be born into great wealth and luxury. It deeply disturbed them that people were starving and living in appalling conditions. They felt that together they could make a difference.

Combining all of their expertise and knowledge, they decided to use their unique position to improve other people's lives. They did marry, and on their honeymoon they traveled the world to bring relief and hope to poverty-stricken areas.

Neither Sleeping Beauty nor her prince wanted to have children. Some people don't. The world was their home, and the people they met along the way became their extended family.

—— ⚘ ——

After I would finish reading one of these stories, I'd close the book and smile. "They all lived realistically ever after," I'd say.

My girls would just lie in their beds, looking at me as if I were crazy. "Gee, Mommy," they'd say, "that's not what it says in the book!"